101 Questions and Answers on Eastern Catholic Churches

101 QUESTIONS AND ANSWERS ON EASTERN CATHOLIC CHURCHES

Edward Faulk

Paulist Press
New York/Mahwah, NJ

Cover design by Cindy Dunne
Book design by Theresa M. Sparacio

Library of Congress Cataloging-in-Publication Data

Faulk, Edward.
   101 questions and answers on Eastern Catholic Churches / Edward Faulk.
     p.   cm.
   ISBN-13: 978-0-8091-4441-9 (alk. paper)
   1. Catholic Church—Oriental rites—Miscellanea. I. Title. II. Title: One hundred and one questions and answers on Eastern Catholic Churches. III. Title: One hundred and one questions and answers on Eastern Catholic Churches.
BX4710.35.F38 2007
281'.5—dc22

                                               2006029218

Published by Paulist Press
997 Macarthur Boulevard
Mahwah, New Jersey 07430

www.paulistpress.com

Printed and bound in the
United States of America

CONTENTS

To my wife Sandy:
her permission was needed for me to be ordained,
and her support and love allow me to serve.

ACKNOWLEDGMENTS

No book is ever developed in a vacuum. Consequently, there is always a need to get input, advice, and help from various people. At the risk of forgetting someone, I'd like to thank my editor, Kevin Carrizo di Camillo, whose patient work turned a manuscript into something worth reading; Bishop Tod David Brown, my Latin bishop, who granted me permission to serve the Melkite Church; Bishop John Elya, who was, at the time, the Eparch of Newton and granted me permission to serve the Melkite Church; and to Archbishop Cyril Bustros, the current eparch, who has allowed me to continue serving.

I want to thank Archimandrite James Babcock, pastor of Holy Cross Melkite Greek Catholic Church, who extended the invitation to me to "come and serve" in the Melkite Church and who has been a great source of information for me; and Father Tim Ramaekers, my Latin pastor, who found a way to spare me for a couple of Sundays a month. For Father Antoine Bakh, pastor of St. John Maron Maronite Church, and all the members of the Eastern Catholic Pastoral Association of Southern California, who have helped me to get a good feel for the depth and breadth of the spirituality and religious practices of the Eastern Catholic Churches.

I would be remiss if I forgot Deacon Irenaeus Dionne, who held my hand and helped me in the early days of my service to the East; and Father Justin Rose, pastor of St. Philip Melkite Mission, who is my spiritual father and whose guidance and help have meant a great deal to me. Finally, I want to thank Dr. Charles Frazee, who read the manuscript and offered numerous corrections and historical tidbits that made this work so much better. Finally, any and all mistakes, omissions, or errors are mine and mine alone.

E.F.
Fullerton, California
January 2006

INTRODUCTION

In the beginning was the Word....
—The Gospel of Saint John the Evangelist 1:1

Every author has to consider the sensibilities of the reader. What is it, dear reader, that you are like? What do you want from this book? What background do you have? I'm going to assume that you are probably a Latin or Roman Catholic (the odds favor this, as there are more than one billion Latin Catholics and about sixteen million Eastern Catholics). I'm also going to assume that you have some interest in the Eastern Catholic Churches.

Of course, you could be an Eastern Catholic and are looking at this book for information about churches other than your own. There's also the possibility that you are reading this just to see what I have to say. Fair enough! I think this book can address all these issues. Why is that?

For the past seven years it has been my great joy to serve as a "bi-ritual" deacon. The term *bi-ritual* means that I have ecclesiastical permission to function as a deacon in both the Roman Catholic Church to which I was ordained and in another church. In this case, the other church is the Melkite Church, one of the Byzantine Churches. In the course of events I have developed a great love for the Eastern Catholic Churches (not just those of the Byzantine Rite) and have studied them out of the simple joy of learning about the developments in the church that Christ founded.

Before we go further, however, we need to have a working vocabulary that will allow us to take this journey of discovery together. Think of this introduction as a primer of important terms.

1. What's the difference between the Eastern Catholic Churches and the Orthodox Church?

The early church (from roughly AD 300 to 600) can be loosely categorized as being composed of two parts: one Western and one Eastern. The Western part is what today is called the "Roman Catholic Church" (this is a popular term that is not precisely correct). The Eastern Churches were not as tightly bound as was the Church of Rome. They developed more as a confederation of churches, working together to ensure that they retained their orthodoxy while keeping their particular forms of worship, style of vestments, and so on.

Following the so-called East-West Schism of 1054, the Churches of the East retained the name *Orthodox* (from the Greek meaning "right glory"), while the Church of Rome retained the title *Catholic* (from the Greek meaning "universal").

In some cases, parts of various Orthodox Churches grew discontented with their treatment at the hands of other Orthodox or local authorities, and they petitioned Rome for union. The first of these was the Chaldean Church[1] and, later, the Union of Brest (1595), which led to a long period of "Uniatism."[2] Those Orthodox Churches that returned to communion with the Church of Rome are part of what we now call "Eastern Catholic Churches." In other cases, there was a strong sense of mission to restore unity with Rome. Other Eastern Catholic Churches have no Orthodox counterpart: the Maronites and the Italo-Albanians.

Liturgically and theologically, the churches that were part of the Orthodox Church are no different from their Orthodox counterparts, with a few exceptions: Eastern Catholic Churches accept the teachings of the Church of Rome that were defined after the Schism of 1054 as being universally binding, although they may express them differently, in keeping with their theological background; in

5

the Liturgy there is a point when the priest commemorates his bishop and, if it is a patriarchal church, his patriarch. At this point, Eastern Catholic Churches commemorate the "Pope of Rome."

Let's take this one step further. The term *Byzantine* simply refers to those churches that follow the liturgical traditions of Byzantium. This includes all the Orthodox Churches and the Byzantine Eastern Catholic Churches. It does not include the Eastern Orthodox that are, generally, Syriac in tradition, nor does it include those Eastern Catholic Churches that follow the Armenian, Chaldean, Coptic, or Syriac Rites (see Question 9 for more on the Byzantine Churches, and Question 12 for more on the other Rites).

2. Does *Rite* mean the same thing as *Church*?

The term *rite* has several meanings. First, a "rite" is a particular *ritual* such as the Mass, baptism, marriage, or even a way of doing something that has become ritualized over time. But it also has a bigger meaning. In the context of this book, it refers to the rituals and customs of particular churches: the way in which they celebrate the Liturgy, the sacraments (or, as they are called in the East, the "mysteries"), and the form of chant that is used in these churches.

In the lower-case form *(rite)*, the term refers to a specific ritual function such as baptism or anointing of the sick. In the capitalized form *(Rite)* it refers to a particular collection of rituals used by one or more churches. And, to complicate this a bit more, there is another sense—the word can be used to indicate a *collection of rites,* such as the Rite of Christian Initiation of Adults (RCIA). In this book we generally talk about "Rite" in the sense of one or more churches. There is another term that we use that should be mentioned in this context. That term is *sui iuris,* which means "in its own right" and refers to the fact that the Eastern Catholic Churches exist "in their own right" as independent churches.

Let's look at an incorrect usage to help put this in perspective. It would be wrong to say "Maronite Rite Church" or "Melkite Rite Church," since the Maronites are technically part of the Syriac Rite and the Melkites are part of the Byzantine Rite.

3. Based upon your answer to Question 1, it seems that we aren't all Roman Catholics. Is that true?

Yes, that's true. The term *Roman Catholic* was first coined by the Church of England (Anglican Church) as a way of distinguishing between themselves (Anglican Catholics) and the Catholics who followed the pope in Rome (Roman Catholics). While this term has never been a part of the official title of the Catholic Church, it can be thought of as synonymous with the more correct term *Latin Rite Church,* which is sometimes shortened to *Latin Church.* So, in the primary meaning, not all Catholics are Roman Catholics.

The second sense, and one commonly used, is that of Catholics who are united with Rome. This sense is technically incorrect but seems to have sufficient popular usage to be addressed here. Most Eastern Catholics would deny that they are "Roman Catholics"—with one significant exception. Members of the Melkite Greek Catholic Church might identify themselves as *Rum Katolique,* which translates, freely, as "Roman Catholic," but it actually refers to the "New Rome" (that is, Constantinople). The Melkites would, however, agree that they are united with Rome and acknowledge the primacy of the Holy Father, the Pope of Rome.

4. What do you mean by "a New Rome"?

This term has been used twice in the history of the church. First, it was used by those who moved to Byzantium with the Roman emperor when he established his new capital there (AD 324). Thus, Byzantium (renamed Constantinople) became the "New Rome" because it was the capital of the eastern part of the Roman Empire.

Still later the term would be used by the Russians who, shortly after the fall of Constantinople in 1453, called Moscow the "New Rome." As an aside, Patriarch Bartholomew (the Orthodox Patriarch of Constantinople, sometimes called the "Ecumenical Patriarch") has recently condemned the idea of Moscow as the Third Rome. Still, the Russian Orthodox Church has held that this position must be maintained because it was prophesized by Saint Seraphim of Sarov. The scope of this book precludes us digging deeper into this issue, so we'll let it go at that.

5. In your answer to Question 2, you used the term *Liturgy* and capitalized it. I've seen this term used in different contexts, so how are you using it here?

Good question! The word *liturgy* comes from two Greek words: *ergon* meaning "work" and *laos* meaning "people." Thus, the term *liturgy* means "the work of the people."

As used here, the term *Liturgy* refers specifically to the formal public prayer of the church. This includes the Mass, the Liturgy of the Hours (what clergy, religious, and some laypersons pray as part of their spiritual or communal life), and other formalized rituals.

Now that we've mentioned the Mass, we probably ought to explain the term *Mass*. In chapter 2 of the Acts of the Apostles[3] we read about the community gathering on the first day of the week for the breaking of the bread. The phrase "breaking of the bread" refers to the celebration of the Eucharist. The formal term for this celebration is the *Liturgy*. In the Latin Church this term was eventually dropped, and the term *Mass* came into common usage based upon the Latin dismissal at the end of the Liturgy: *Ite missa est* (which is freely translated as "Go, the Mass is ended"). In the Eastern Churches that follow the Byzantine tradition, the generally accepted term is *Divine Liturgy*. Churches that follow the Syriac tradition tend to use the word *Qorbono,* a Syriac word meaning "to offer," or *Quddas,* an Arabic word meaning "to make holy." Chaldean Catholics have adopted the term *Mass* for their Liturgy, as do the Syro-Malabar and Syro-Malankara Churches.

Later in the book, we provide greater detail on these churches and explain more about the Divine Liturgy (see Question 7).

6. How many people are in the Eastern Catholic Churches?

This is a difficult question to answer because, as with the Roman Catholic Church, not everybody stands up to be counted, and some are counted who, while claiming to be Catholic, do not actually *practice* the faith or attend Liturgy on a regular basis. Table 1 provides reasonably accurate numbers as of the time this book was written.

Table 1   Membership of Eastern Catholic Churches

Albanian Byzantine Catholic Church	3,000
Armenian Church	368,923
Bulgarian Byzantine Catholic Church	10,000
Chaldean Church	382,637
Coptic Church	242,513
Eastern Catholic Churches (without Hierarchy)	65,000
Ethiopian/Eritrean (Ge'ez) Church	196,858
Greek Byzantine Catholic Church	2,345
Greek Catholics in former Yugoslavia	76,670
Hungarian Byzantine Catholic Church	268,935
Italo-Albanian Byzantine Catholic Church	60,448
Maronite Church	3,106,792
Melkite Greek Catholic Church	1,340,913
Romanian Greek Catholic Church	746,000
Ruthenian Byzantine Catholic Church	597,623

Table 1   *Continued*

Slovak Greek Catholic Church	225,136
Syrian Church	123,376
Syro-Malabar Church	3,752,432
Syro-Malankara Church	404,052
Ukrainian Greek Catholic Church	4,321,508

In round numbers, then, the Eastern Catholics are just over sixteen million in number around the world.

7. Roman Catholics have the Mass as their central form of worship. Do Eastern Catholics have the Mass as well?

For Roman Catholics, the eucharistic celebration is the central form of worship; they call this "the Mass." All Eastern Catholics have a eucharistic celebration as the primary focus of their liturgical life. (In Question 5 we touched upon the Mass and the Eastern equivalent.) There is a difference, however, in the liturgical life of Eastern Catholics and that of their Latin brothers and sisters.

In general, when Roman Catholics gather to celebrate a Liturgy it is to have the Mass. Eastern Catholics, however, do not. There is a rich and varied liturgical life to be found in the East; the Divine Liturgy (or *Qorbono,* Mass, *Quddas*) forms the hub around which the rest revolves. Vespers, Matins, and Orthros (a combination of Matins and Lauds) are weekly staples for many Eastern Catholics. In fact, Eastern Catholics can meet their "obligation" for attending church on Sunday by going to Saturday night vespers. (See Question 38.)

Roman Catholics may pray the Liturgy of the Hours (see Question 5) either as individuals or in a group. Since Liturgy is never a private prayer, it is preferable that the Liturgy of the Hours be prayed in a group (called "communal prayer"), but because of necessity individual prayer is fairly frequent. The Liturgies that form the Liturgy of the Hours include Morning Prayer (Lauds), Evening Prayer (Vespers), and the Office of Readings (Matins). There is also Night Prayer and Daytime Prayer (the latter may be said at three different times, mid-morning, noon, and mid-afternoon).

ONE

THE CHURCHES

Where the Church is, there is the treasure
of the unutterable Mysteries.
—Saint John Chrysostom, *Homily XIV on First Corinthians*

8. Is it true that language and nationality are the primary reason for so many different Eastern Catholic (and Orthodox) Churches?

To a certain extent, both language and culture played a role in the development of the Eastern Churches, both Catholic and Orthodox. As the gospel was spread at the beginning of the church, the apostles and disciples who shared the good news worked hard to enculturate the message, to show how it fit within the lives of those who heard it. Saint Paul, in his famous speech to the Athenians (Acts 17:22–25)[4] made reference to the "unknown god" and explained that we know whom we worship— he took what they already had and fit the gospel to it.

For this reason there is a local tie-in to the Scriptures by the church. Over time this developed into what we would today see as a group of national churches. Exceptions to this "accidental" process include Armenia, the first Christian country (the entire country followed their king in accepting Christianity, possibly as early as 301 but certainly no later than 314). Russia, too, would be motivated by its leaders who embraced Eastern Christianity after they sent emissaries to Constantinople. Upon their return they claimed that they "knew not if we were on earth or in heaven" in reference to the Liturgy. As a result of their report, the Russian Orthodox Church was established. It followed the Byzantine Rite and, eventually, established many of its own traditions, such as the use of language and hymnody.

Other regions also "customized" their worship styles. The local churches used the language of the people, which has always been a tradition in the Eastern Churches. In cases where there were multiple languages, one eventually became the "holy" language that was used in the church. Thus, for example, Old Church Slavonic became the default language used in both the Russian and Ruthenian Churches, even though this language is no longer in common usage. In the Roman Church, Greek, and later Latin, became the official language of the Latin Church.

So, we can look at the situation today and suppose that the churches have a national character and language, but that is really the result of their development rather than the goal of their establishment.

9. You mentioned "Byzantine Churches." What are they? Also, the term *Churches* is plural—there's more than one of them?

The Byzantine Churches are those churches that follow the Byzantine liturgical practices. These practices grew and developed primarily in and around Constantinople, originally called "Byzantium" (today Istanbul in Turkey), and thus the source of their name. Even though the city was renamed in the fourth century, the ritual name remains. Most noticeable of these practices are the two major Divine Liturgies that are used, those of Saint John Chrysostom and Saint Basil. A third liturgy, that of the Presanctified, is found in all Byzantine Churches, but it is actually derived primarily from the work of Pope Saint Gregory the Great. This Presanctified Liturgy is also found in a modified form in the Latin Church and is used on Good Friday for the communion service and for *Sunday Celebrations in the Absence of a Priest*— a "communion service".

The reason the term *Churches* is plural is that there are fourteen churches that use the Byzantine Rite. We address this question a little more later on, but for now, here's a list of the Byzantine Rite Churches: Albanian, Bulgarian, Byelorussian, Croatian, Georgian, Greek, Hungarian, Italo-Albanian, Melkite, Romanian, Russian, Ruthenian, Slovakian and Ukrainian. Although they all use the same Byzantine Rite, there may be small differences among them. These differences, called "recensions," are based upon the development of the Liturgy within each community. The overall structures, and indeed even most of the fine points, are identical other than language and musical style.

Language in the Eastern Churches has traditionally been that of the people, although certain "sacred language" concepts have developed among various churches. Musical styling and settings are also subject to the culture in which the church finds herself. Thus, the Russian settings are different from, say, the Arabic settings of the Melkite Church.

10. What would happen to the Eastern Catholic Churches if there is "reunion" with the Orthodox?

If there should be a reunion, it is expected that the Eastern Catholic Churches would rejoin the corresponding Orthodox Church. Thus, for example, the Melkites would rejoin the Antiochians, the Greek Catholics would rejoin the Greek Orthodox, and the Russian Catholics would rejoin the Russian Orthodox.

There are areas of concern remaining with some of the Eastern Catholic Churches. For example, the Ukrainian and Ruthenian Churches would, technically, rejoin the Russian Church, but there are political considerations that might enter into such a decision. One would hope that if we have resolved the issues that separate the Catholic and Orthodox Churches, we could certainly address these political issues.

Those churches that have no corresponding Orthodox Church would remain separate entities or, as the church sees them today, *sui iuris* churches.

The term *reunion* also needs to be properly understood. It does not mean that the Orthodox Churches would become part of the Latin Rite—they would remain as independent churches, but they would be *in communion* with Rome and, consequently, Rome would be in communion with them. As used here, the expression "in communion" means more than simply accepting and sharing the sacrament; it means that we profess the same faith (albeit with possibly different terms). Thus, the term *reunion* is more precise than *rejoin,* since history shows that the churches we now call "Orthodox" were never a part of the Latin Catholic Church but were, in fact, churches in their own right, sharing a common faith and sacraments with the Church of Rome.

11. What is the relationship between the Eastern Catholic Churches and the Orthodox Church?

In general, the Eastern Catholic Churches are portions of the Orthodox Churches that broke off for one or more reasons and came into communion with the Roman Catholic Church. The exceptions are the Italo-Albanian Church and the Maronites. The Italo-Albanian Church was founded in Italy and remained there, never breaking communion with the Roman Catholic Church. Tradition holds that the Maronites, too, were never out of communion with Rome even though they were located in the Middle East.

Because the Eastern Catholic Churches did break away from the Orthodox Churches and, thereby, broke communion with their "mother Church," it follows that there is some tension between them. Working relations between them tend to be good, especially in areas where the two can support charitable outreach missions.

In the Middle East, the relationship between the Melkite and Antiochian Churches is less strained. In fact, a degree of (unofficial) intercommunion is found there. Since small villages might have only a Melkite or an Antiochian parish, the people from any given village simply go to the church that is there. If they are in another village, they will go to that church, and whether it is Orthodox or Catholic doesn't seem to enter into the picture.

This has led some Melkite bishops to take a leading role in trying to find a common ground for reunion. One such proposal, rejected by both Rome and the Orthodox, was that the Melkite Church come into communion with both Orthodoxy *and* Rome, which would allow the Melkites to form a bridge. This role of bridge builder is, in fact, one that the Melkites have taken on.

Melkite patriarchs have consistently said that they are the voice of the Orthodox in Rome.

12. How do the Eastern Catholic Churches differ from *each other?*

To answer this question we have to treat the differences among the churches of a given Rite and then look at the differences among the Rites. Having said that, let's see what we can address.

As we noted in Question 9, there are differences of language, musical settings, and some minor liturgical variations in the churches of the Byzantine Rite. The same is true for all of the other Rites except the Armenian. Since the Armenian *Church* and the Armenian *Rite* are one and the same, it follows that there are no variations there.

Within the Syriac Rite, the Maronites have a particular liturgy that itself varies by season of the year and is different from the Syro-Malabar and Syro-Malankara Churches. The latter two, both Indian Churches, are very similar and differ in virtually nothing. Historical records of these two churches have been lost, but attempts are currently being made to reconstruct the Liturgy of the early church.

The Alexandrian Churches are quite different, but primarily for cultural reasons. The Ge'ez Church found in Ethiopia uses the Alexandrian Rite, which derives from the Divine Liturgy of Saint Mark. However, the church uses the ancient language of Ethiopia called *Ge'ez*. Historical records for this church have, sadly, been lost, and it is impossible to reconstruct the earliest form of worship there. The Coptic Catholic Church uses a liturgy that is a modified version of the Divine Liturgy of Saint Basil.

Beyond these minor differences, there are differences of government based upon the type of church—whether it has a patriarch, a metropolitan archbishop, or no head at all.

Theologically, there are no differences, although, again, there may be a "difference of expression," meaning that how something is explained may differ from church to church.

13. When you say in Question 11 that the Maronites were never "out of communion" with Rome, what does that mean?

As we've already seen, following the Schism of 1054, the Orthodox Churches slowly broke communion with the Church of Rome. There were two churches that never broke communion and that do not have Orthodox counterparts. These are the Italo-Albanian Church located in Italy and the Maronite Church, which today is primarily located in Lebanon.

The origins of the Maronite Church can be reconstructed only with some difficulty. Following the Council of Chalcedon (AD 451), there were arguments between the Monophysites and the Chalcedonians. It is certainly true that a community grew up in the mountain region of Lebanon under the leadership of Saint John Maron, who had been elected the first patriarch of the Maronites.

While tradition holds that they never "broke communion" with Rome, they were out of contact with Rome until Patriarch Jeremiah brought his group into contact with the Crusaders. Later he came to the Lateran Council in 1215. This was a direct result of the "rediscovery" of the Maronites during the Crusades. In fact, there is a famous painting of Jeremiah celebrating Mass there that was commissioned by Pope Innocent III and restored by Pope Innocent XIII. So, while they were never "out of communion," they were most certainly out of contact.

14. There's an Eastern Catholic Church near us whose members are Arabs. Who are they?

Arab Christians are mostly members of the Melkite or Maronite Churches, but some may be members of the Chaldean Church found in Iraq and Iran.

Christianity is a religion that finds its origins in the Middle East. Many of the early converts to Christianity were, in fact, people whom today are known as Arabs. Large concentrations of Arab Christians populated the Middle East until the establishment of the Muslims. Even today there are large groups of Arab Christians in Jordan, Syria, Lebanon, Egypt, and Palestine.

Many Arab Christians have migrated to other parts of the world. They are found on virtually every continent and in every country. In the United States, large groups of Arab Christians are found in Southern California, Michigan (especially around Detroit), and New England. Smaller groups are present in virtually every major city.

Because the Eastern Catholic Churches are not as prevalent as the Roman Catholic Church, many Arab Christians attend Latin Masses instead of going to the Eastern or Syriac Church of which they are members.

15. Do the Eastern Catholic Churches use Latin, or do they use English or some other language?

Latin is the theological and liturgical language of the Roman Catholic Church, but it is not used in other Catholic Churches. In general, Eastern Churches use the language of the people where they are located. Thus, Arabic is used in Arab countries, French is used in French-speaking lands, and English is used in America, England, and other English-speaking places.

There are "sacred languages" used in the Eastern Churches that function much as Latin does in the Roman Catholic Church. Among these are Old Church Slavonic, used in the Russian, Ukrainian, and Ruthenian Churches; Ge'ez, used in the Church of Ethiopia; and Greek, which is found to some degree in virtually all of the Eastern Catholic Churches.

16. I attended a Catholic Church in Washington, DC. They seem different from any of the Eastern or Western Catholic Churches. Who are they?

Congratulations! You have found the only Ge'ez Church in the United States! This church serves the Ethiopians and Eritreans (Eritrea is just north of Ethiopia on the east side of Africa) found in and around the Washington, D.C., area. This particular church is part of an ancient tradition. Saint Athanasius, the Patriarch of Alexandria, sent Saint Frumentius to Aksum in Ethiopia, where he was the first bishop. He brought with him the Divine Liturgy of Saint Mark, which became the basis for Ethiopian liturgical practice. As was typical of all Eastern Churches, Ethiopian chants developed a local influence—in this case from the gifted musician, Saint Yared.

17. My sister-in-law's family is Eastern Catholic, but they're from Italy. How is that possible?

The Italo-Albanian Church is an Eastern Catholic Church in an area of Italy that was settled by Albanians. Because they brought their Byzantine traditions with them, they continued to worship in the Eastern tradition. But that's just part of the story. The southern part of Italy and most of Sicily had ties to Greece, and from the very beginnings of Christianity, Byzantine communities flourished there. Because this area was, geographically, part of the Latin Church, a slow but inevitable process of incorporation into the Latin Church took place. However, in the eighth century, the Byzantine Emperor Leo III removed the area from Latin authority and placed it under Constantinople while not replacing the bishops. This led to an almost immediate resurgence of Byzantine practices, and dozens of Byzantine monasteries developed along the coast.

But all was not to remain so comfortable. In the eleventh century the Normans conquered this part of Italy and moved it back under Latin control. Byzantine practices were discouraged, and Byzantine bishops were replaced by Latin bishops. Once again, a process of latinization took place.

With the arrival of two groups of Albanians in the fifteenth century, there was yet another swing of the pendulum. Those Albanians who were Latin Catholics were simply absorbed into the Latin Church, while those who were Orthodox retained their own traditions, and a third resurgence of Byzantine practice took hold. This resurgence was bolstered by the publication of the papal bull *Etsi pastoralis,* which protected the Italo-Albanian Church, established the equality of the Byzantine and Latin Rites, and set the stage for further developments, especially those seen under the pontificate of Pope John Paul II of blessed memory.

18. I sometimes hear the term *Greek Catholic.* Is that the same as *Greek Orthodox?*

No. The terms *Catholic* and *Orthodox* set them apart. At present, the Catholic Church and the Orthodox Church are not in communion with one another. To make things more complex, however, the term *Greek Catholic* has multiple meanings. It may refer to the very small Eastern Catholic Church in Greece, or it may refer to any of the Eastern Catholic Churches of the Byzantine Rite! If you were to visit my Melkite parish you would see a sign that proclaims "Holy Cross Melkite-Greek Catholic Church." Here the use of the word *Greek* does not mean the parish is made up of Greeks (although there are some) but, rather, that the parish follows the Byzantine tradition. In fact, most Byzantine Churches retain some Greek in their liturgies, even though it may be as minor as it is in the Roman Catholic Church—the expressions *Kyrie eleison* ("Lord have mercy") and *Christe eleison* ("Christ have mercy") are Greek.

19. My family was Eastern Catholic, but when we came to the United States we settled in an area where there were no Eastern Catholic Churches, so we started going to the Latin Church. Does that make us Roman Catholics?

No. One of the marvelous things about the Catholic Church is that Catholic is Catholic. A Catholic can go to any Catholic Church regardless of Rite and receive the sacraments or mysteries there. The Rite to which one belongs is a function of the Rite to which your father belonged. If your father were, for example,

Ukrainian, then you are a Ukrainian regardless of where you were baptized (assuming, of course, that you were baptized in a Catholic Church).

Simply attending a different *ritual* church does not change your *Rite*. That requires specific action on your part, and on the bishops involved. Changing ritual churches is not something that one undertakes without serious and deep consideration. First, it can normally only be done once. Second, you must normally reside in and be active in the ritual church to which you wish to belong for a substantial period of time (usually several years) before a petition to change churches would even be considered.

Typical reasons for changing ritual churches involve such things as a deep love for, and spiritual nourishment by, the other church, along with an intention to live out the spiritual life of that church. Many of the priests that I work with in the Eastern Churches did, in fact, grow up as Latin Rite Catholics who, because of their love for the East, changed ritual churches and later entered into the seminary to study for the priesthood.

Let me share one anecdote with you about what can happen when one thinks one has changed ritual churches (or never knew one was a member of a different ritual church) because of long-standing attendance at a Roman Catholic Church. My predecessor deacon in the Melkite parish I serve was ordained as a Latin Rite deacon. When he was asked to serve the Melkites, he petitioned for bi-ritual faculties. In doing the necessary research it was discovered that he was actually a member of the Italo-Albanian Church. His family had been attending the Latin Rite Church for so long that he didn't even know that! Such things happen, and the church generally doesn't worry about them too much.

TWO

HISTORY

Practical knowledge is distributed among many subjects and interests, but theoretical is divided into two parts, i.e., the historical interpretation and the spiritual sense.
— Saint John Cassian, *The Conferences,* The First Conference of Abbot Nesteros, Chapter VIII: Of Spiritual Knowledge

20. I was taught that Jesus established one church, but it doesn't seem that you agree. How many churches did Jesus establish?

Jesus established *one* church. There are, however, many *expressions* of that church. Those of us who grew up with the *Baltimore Catechism* learned that there are four "marks" of the church: she is one, holy, catholic, and apostolic. In this case, even though we talk about "churches" in the plural, there is One Church because we share one faith, one baptism, one Lord. Each of the Eastern Catholic Churches agrees to share the sacraments (or, as they are called in the East, "mysteries") with members of any other Catholic Church.

The multiplicity of churches is simply the way in which the gospel of Christ has been spread and lived in different places by people with different customs and traditions.

This may seem strange for members of the Roman Catholic Church who have thought that they alone were Catholic. Yet, even in the Roman Catholic Church we have seen different practices that grew in one area and sometimes spread to other areas and other times not.

This is similar to the way in which the different churches that form the One Church have developed. Julius Caesar begins his *Gallic Wars* by commenting that "all of Gaul is divided into three parts....These differ from each other in language, customs, and laws." We can see a similar reality in the church—there is one church, but she has many parts differentiated by language, customs, and even canon (church) law.

21. Well, if there was just one church, how did we get so many expressions of it?

As we noted previously, there is just one church, but there are many expressions of that church. To fully understand this situation we have to go back to the time of the apostles and work forward. When Paul went around preaching the good news, he established local churches (the word he uses is the Greek term *ekklesia,* meaning "the community called out"). By the close of the first century, the churches each had a type of structure in which a bishop (Greek: *episkopos*) was in charge. There were priests *(presbyteroi)* and deacons *(diakonoi)* to assist the bishop. The development of this structure is clearly described by Saint Ignatius of Antioch in letters he wrote on his way to martyrdom in Rome.[5]

These "city churches" communicated with Paul via letters (most of which have been lost) and with each other. Most of the letters of Paul that we retain in Scripture are his responses to these letters in which he corrects problems or offers encouragement to the local communities.

As time went by, the churches in local regions began to associate with each other and with a metropolitan—a bishop who headed a particular geographic region and in the sixth century became known as a "patriarch." The "pentarchy" was composed of the five major Sees or, as the Latin Church calls them, "Dioceses." These were Rome, Constantinople, Alexandria, Antioch, and Jerusalem. Issues that arose within the churches of these patriarchal Sees were addressed by the patriarch and the synod of bishops. When a problem crossed boundaries, Rome was invited to resolve the difference or, if the problem was big enough, an ecumenical council was called.

Within each of these patriarchates, local churches retained their status of individual churches. So, for example, Constantinople lead the Greek Church and, later, the Russian Church until the close of the sixteenth century. Antioch would eventually develop into five different churches, and so on. Eventually there were twenty-two (or, perhaps, twenty-three) churches that were identified as churches in their own right.

22. So there are twenty-two churches. Does that include the Orthodox Churches?

The short answer is no, it does not. We should also clarify a point that the Orthodox make: The term *Orthodox Church* is singular. Like the Catholic Church, the Orthodox Church is made up of numerous churches, but because they profess *one* faith, *one* baptism, and share the mysteries (what Latin Catholics call "sacraments"), they really are a single church.

Now, having said that, it's important to note that popes down through history, including Pope Benedict XVI, have worked toward a reunion of the Catholic and Orthodox Churches so that we can truly represent Christ with *one* mind and *one* church.

23. Does this have anything to do with the Great Schism of 1054?

First, let's disabuse ourselves of the idea that 1054 was a magic year. It was, in fact, the year nothing happened! Let's examine the history of this event so that we can understand what the reality is.

The Great Schism was not the first schism between East and West. As we've already noted, relations between the East and the West had been strained for a long time. Theological differences were understood to be, primarily, a matter of expression and were not the focal point of the friction that was taking place, although the insertion of the *filioque* (the phrase "and the son") into the Creed (at the local Council of Toledo in 589 and about 1000 in Rome) had antagonized the Eastern Church. Sources of friction were found in practices and in political actions taken by the East and the West. Among the practices that were different were the ordination of married men in the East and the use of unleavened bread for holy communion in the West. There was also an issue of language when it came to communications between the two: the West used Latin and the East used Greek. Actions taken by both East and West included the closing of parish churches and the replacement of clergy from one church with those of the other.

The so-called Photian Schism took place during the ninth century. This schism set the stage for what was to follow.

The tradition of both the East and the West was that, in general, territory evangelized by a particular church belonged to that church. The best example of that was Russia. Russia was evangelized by the church in Constantinople and, therefore, it became an Eastern Church under the authority of Constantinople (it was later granted "autocephalous" status, meaning that it was a separate church).

The Photian Schism involved Bulgaria, which was originally evangelized by the Greeks (Constantinople), who applied pressure on the Bulgarian ruler, Boris I, to accept a Greek bishop. The problem was that Boris I wanted an autocephalous bishop, and this was not granted. He, therefore, turned to Rome. Rome sent a bishop to Bulgaria who infuriated Photius, the Patriarch of Constantinople. Photius called a council and condemned the actions of Rome, excommunicating Pope Nicholas I, who died before he could respond. Later Photius was deposed by the Byzantine emperor, and Pope Hadrian in turn excommunicated Photius. To make this even more confusing, Rome did not satisfy the expectations of the Bulgarians, who returned to the Greek fold under Constantinople.

By the eleventh century, the Church of Rome was no longer fluent in Greek, and many of the senior prelates, especially Cardinal Humbert, had developed distrust for anything the Greeks (the Eastern Churches) did. On the other side, Michael Cerularius had become the patriarch after a career as a civil servant. He did not have extensive theological training, nor was he a particularly skilled diplomat. Cerularius had a very low opinion of the papacy (but not of the pope himself), so he and Humbert were diametrically opposed to each other.

Nevertheless, when in 1054 word of the problems the Byzantines had in Southern Italy arrived in Constantinople, Cerularius wrote to Pope Leo IX asking for clarification. The letter was written in Greek, and Cardinal Humbert himself translated it. We do not know if the translation was accurate or not, nor do we know how well Humbert spoke Greek. In any event, Cerularius addressed the letter to the pope as "Brother" rather than using the more traditional title of "Father" and compounded the insult by signing it as the "Ecumenical Patriarch," the title the pope at that time applied to himself.

Humbert convinced the pope to send legates to Constantinople to address this situation. He himself wrote two letters, one to Cerularius and one to the emperor, Constantine IX (Monomachus). The emperor received the letter from Humbert with equanimity, but the clergy in Constantinople did not. In fact, the reception of the legates, which included Humbert, was so lacking in protocol that Humbert did not even greet Cerularius but simply handed him the letter. Cerularius, for his part, was taken aback by this action, which seemed so unlike Pope Leo.

After reading the letter, one of the Byzantine monks wrote a rebuttal in which he condemned the Roman practices of celibate clergy, the use of unleavened bread, and other practices. Humbert fired off an ill-tempered response to the monk and even questioned the orthodoxy of a church that refused to use the *filioque!* Cerularius, for his part, simply ignored the legates. This so infuriated Humbert that he and the other legates entered Hagia Sophia, the great church in Constantinople, just before the start of the Liturgy and tossed a bull of excommunication on the holy table (altar). This letter excommunicated Cerularius, Constantine IX, and all their followers. They then left. Since Pope Leo had died before this action took place, Humbert was technically "without canonical mission," meaning that his action had no force of law and he was without authority to do what he did. Contained in this bull were lists of "offenses," some of which were true, but others were not.

Cerularius, in return, excommunicated Humbert and the other two legates. This might have been rectified on their return to Rome except that one of the legates, Frederick of Loraine, was soon to become Pope Stephen X. Pope Victor II, who reigned between the papacy of Leo and Stephen, did not address the issue. So, the excommunications remained, and popular interpretation made them more powerful than they really were.

However, communion between the churches was not broken by this event. Relations remained strained, but tolerable.

24. In Question 23, you said the year 1054 was "the year nothing happened." Why, then, are the events of that year recognized as pivotal for the Great Schism?

As we noted, the actions of 1054 did not break communion between the churches and, consequently, did not affect the break (schism) between the churches. The Church in Rome remained in communion with the Russian Church and other Eastern Churches for more than three hundred years after the events of 1054. However, the strain that these events placed on the relations between the East and West can be said to be the trigger that began a long series of events that would eventually lead to the breaking of relations and severing of communion between the Churches of the West and the Churches of the East.

Perhaps the excommunications that had been levied were perceived to be of a broader scope than they really were. It is also possible that the events of 1054 were seen in the context of all that would later happen and, therefore, this date was pinpointed as the date of the schism. This was first noted in the work of the English historian Edward Gibbon.

Regardless of why the date was chosen, most historians no longer consider 1054 to be the exact date when the Great East-West Schism began.

25. How did the Eastern Churches come about?

Following the Great Schism, the Orthodox Churches slowly broke communion with the Church of Rome. Rome for the most part ignored them. Eventually, however, political situations, the Crusades, and Jesuit evangelization would change that.

We've already seen that tradition holds that the Maronites never broke communion with Rome but were "lost" to Rome because of their reclusiveness in Lebanon. They were "rediscovered" by missionaries. The Italo-Albanian Church remained tied to Rome, although again relegated to the backwaters.

The political situation, both civil and ecclesiastical, in the area of Lithuania and Poland led to the so-called Union of Brest (1595), in which the Ukrainian Church came into communion with Rome at their own request. The Jesuits, who helped bring this about, were disappointed, as they had wanted the Ukrainians to convert directly to the Latin Church.

In India, during the sixteenth century, the Portuguese Jesuits brought about a semi-forced conversion of the St. Thomas Christians (Syro-Malabar and Syro-Malankara) into the Latin Church. This did not last long, however, as some people rejected the idea of being forced to lose their heritage. Eventually the Eastern Churches divided into Catholic and Orthodox Syro-Malabar and Syro-Malankara communities.

Catholics also proselytized Egypt, leading a small number of Copts (Orthodox Coptic Church) into communion with Rome. At the same time, in 1626 some Ethiopians came into communion with Rome.

The Melkites went through a slightly different process. There the issue was the election of a pro-Roman patriarch, which eventually led to a split (circa 1724) within the church, and the Catholic Melkites came into communion with Rome, while the Antiochians remained separated.

This practice of evangelizing and incorporating small Orthodox groups became known as "uniatism."

26. How do the Eastern Churches relate to the Orthodox Church?

There are two ways to approach this question, and we'll address both of them. With two notable exceptions—Italo-Albanian Church and the Maronites—the Eastern Catholic Churches are "children" of the Orthodox Church from which they originated.

In terms of their current relationship with the Orthodox, the question is more complex. The general consensus of the Orthodox laity is that the Eastern Catholics are no longer "graced," meaning that they have separated themselves from the source of grace, which is the Orthodox Church. Further, they have compromised their teachings by accepting Latin teachings that developed after the seventh ecumenical council (Nicaea, 787), the last recognized by the Orthodox.

If we eliminate theological issues, there are still differences that caused strained relationships. Among these were the tendency of some of the Eastern Catholic Churches to adopt Latin practices such as first communions, eucharistic benediction, praying the rosary, elimination of the iconostasis and icons, the use of statues and Western-style clerical vestments. Most of these issues are currently being resolved, since the Second Vatican Council directed Eastern Catholic Churches to return to their authentic heritage.

One final area that we will mention is the perception that Rome "meddles" in the affairs of the Eastern Catholic Churches. That is, the fact that Rome claims a "juridic (legal) authority" over the Eastern Catholic Churches bothers the Orthodox who do not want to grant *any* such authority to Rome. Examples of this "meddling" are in fact relatively rare. One such case occurred during the final years of life of Patriarch Maximos V (1908–2001) of the Melkites. He was too ill to run the church, but the synod of bishops was reluctant to appoint an administrator. Eventually, Pope John Paul II stepped in and called an exceptional synod of the bishops; they, with the encouragement of Rome, selected Archbishop John Haddad of Tyre, Lebanon, as the patriarchal administrator (June 12, 2000). While this was a perfectly benign example, the Orthodox feared that this could lead to something far more sinister.

From the Catholic standpoint, any such fear has been mitigated by years of seeing only positive actions by Rome. At the same time, while history has shown that the popes have generally taken a very positive attitude toward the Eastern Churches, the same has *not* been true for the curia and Latin bishops. There was, for example, the long-standing "agreement" that Eastern Catholics would not have married priests serving in the United States and Canada. This was to appease the Latin bishops who felt that married priests would be a source of scandal. It was also a compromise that came out of a problem that arose with Archbishop John Ireland, whose refusal in 1889 to accept Father Alexis Toth, a widower, led to a sizeable group of Eastern Catholics going over to the Orthodox. This story is quite well known, and in fact the Orthodox consider Father Toth to be a saint (he was canonized at St. Tikhon's Monastery in South Canaan, Pennsylvania, in 1994).

27. I read once that the term *pope* was applied to many people. Why was that?

The word *pope* comes from the Greek word *pappas,* which means "papa" and is used in the same context as the Aramaic and Hebrew word *abba,* translated as "daddy." It was common in the church to call those who were spiritual fathers "Father" or the equivalent term in the language of the people. Because this relationship was quite close in the early church, the term used was almost always the familiar, and for this reason the word *pope* was applied to most deacons, priests, and bishops of the early church. As time went by, its use was replaced by the word *bishop* (*Sayedna* in Arabic or *Mar* in many languages). Today the term is used by the Patriarch of the West, the pope; and by the Patriarch of Alexandria, the head of the Coptic Orthodox Church.

28. Why was the break with the Orthodox Church considered different from that of the Anglican or other churches?

With the split between the Catholics and Orthodox we had a fundamental rupture in the church. The two aspects of East and West were, in many ways, a sort of "checks and balances" that helped the church to remain on an even keel. In a sense, it was the experiential (Orthodox) and the intellectual (Catholic) being separated. Both aspects were (and are) needed. This was not the first such split—there had been many smaller ones prior to this—but it was the first of such a sweeping nature. We must also be careful in attempting to distinguish the West as solely "intellectual" and the East as solely "experiential," since both aspects are present in the East and in the West.

The Anglican (or, the Church of England) split was, at first, simply a *political* split. However, it developed into much more. There was a change in emphasis in the role of the priest and the role of the laity that eventually led Pope Leo XIII to declare Anglican orders (holy orders) to be invalid.[6] This contrasts with the Orthodox, who have retained valid orders and apostolic succession in the eyes of the Church of Rome.

Perhaps the best way to consider this is that the Anglican split was more akin to the schisms that took place following the major councils, when smaller groups broke from the main body of the church, while the Orthodox-Catholic split was more like an earthquake that split a town in half.

29. Why did the reunion of Catholic and Orthodox promulgated at the Council of Florence (1439) fail?

The short answer is that it failed because the laity of the Orthodox Church did not agree to the reunion. Unlike the Catholic Church, which functions in a top-down fashion, the Orthodox Church is often driven from the bottom up.

The Orthodox willingly came to Florence with great hope, but little expectation that they would be treated as they felt they should be. During the council, the Patriarch of Constantinople, who was leading the Orthodox representatives, died. A copy of his journal or diary was found near him. In this diary he allegedly wrote that he accepted all that the Roman Catholic Church taught and believed, especially the *filioque* and papal jurisdiction. Most scholars have since rejected this, claiming that it was contrary to his position as stated a few days before his death, and also that the way in which it was written was inconsistent with Orthodox theology.

Upon the death of the patriarch, Emperor John Paleologos took over the lead role. This was not the first time the emperor had "guided" the Byzantine Church and was not totally unexpected. Eventually, most of the hierarchs signed the agreement, which, in the opinion of many, "sold out" the Orthodox Church. Only Mark of Ephesus (died AD 1452 and later an Orthodox saint) refused to sign. He took an active role in leading the opposition, even to the point of making a deathbed request of his disciple, Gregory, to continue to teach true orthodoxy. The agreement was signed, in large part, because of the threat to Constantinople by the Muslim Turks. The pope had agreed to send troops as well as a Crusade to provide support for the city.

After the Orthodox delegation returned to their homes, the laity began to look at the agreement that had been placed before them. This agreement admitted that the Latins could continue to use the *filioque* but also insisted on papal primacy. Because of this, it was rejected by the people and, in response to this, by the patriarch Gennadios (George Scholarios), who was the disciple of Mark of Ephesus and became the patriarch following the fall of Constantinople.

30. I've heard the term *uniate*. What does it mean and where did it come from?

The term *uniate* was originally applied and is still in use by the Orthodox in a negative sense. It refers to the Eastern Catholic

Churches who had unified themselves with Rome at the expense of their union with the Orthodox Church.

This term more commonly used is *uniatism,* which was the designation for how the Church of Rome brought portions of the Orthodox Churches into communion. Uniatism has since been determined to be the wrong approach—and wrong term—to seeking reunion with the Orthodox and is no longer pursued by the Church of Rome.

31. What is the Balamand Agreement and what significance does it hold for us today?

The Balamand Agreement came out of the joint Catholic-Orthodox dialogue that has been going on for many years. The normal dialogue was set aside to deal with the issue of uniatism (see Question 30). This took place at the Balamand School of Theology in Lebanon during June 1993. Representatives of most of the Orthodox Churches met with representatives of the Catholic Church to discuss this issue.

As a result of their discussions, a short document was produced. This document, called the *Balamand Agreement,* lays out several important principles. First was that the Eastern Catholic Churches, regardless of how they came into being, have a right to exist. Second, the practice of uniatism or seeking reunion by "annexing" portions of the Orthodox Churches was wrong and was not to be pursued by the Catholic Church in the future. As was noted in the agreement, the process of uniatism did not grow unilaterally from the Catholic Church but was, rather, a response to various situations that are beyond the scope of this book.

The agreement also specifies that historically there have been many attempts at reunion, but none have been successful and some have even made things worse. Yet, the unity of Christianity is still a high priority because it reflects the prayer of Christ.

Now, this all sounds fine and good, but there are numerous issues. Not all Orthodox accepted this agreement. Among the issues they raised are the apparent unilateral agreement entered into by the ecumenical patriarch (the Bishop of Constantinople), the rejection of the idea that the church is split in two, and other lesser issues.

We have to remember that the ecumenical patriarch is not the "pope" of the Orthodox. He is the *first* among *equals,* which gives him a primacy of honor, but does not grant him juridic (legal) authority over the other Orthodox Churches, nor does it give him the right to unilaterally speak for the other Orthodox Churches.

The other issue, that of the "split" of Christianity, is a sensitive one for the Orthodox. There are those who hold that the true church is the Orthodox Church and all who are not Orthodox are "without grace," meaning they are not part of the church. Even the more moderate position of the Orthodox is that they know where grace is (in the Orthodox Church), but they do not know where grace is not. Consequently, they do not know if the Catholic Church has grace (is valid) or not.

In respect to the second part of the question, what effect this agreement has on us today, the answer is that it is simply another attempt to resolve an issue that, seemingly, defies all attempts. While the Balamand Agreement lays out what appear to be valid and constructive guidelines for ongoing dialogue, it is not, in and of itself, terribly useful for the resolution of the thousand-year-long schism.

32. There are so many problems in Russia today with the Russian Orthodox Church and the Catholic Church. Are these caused by the historical split of the churches or by something else?

The Russian Church was the last of the Orthodox to break communion with Rome. There was no actual documented break, but, rather, intercommunion slowly faded away. Thus, problems that we see today are really not directly related to the historical separation, although they are not divorced from those events. Looking at the problem dispassionately, we can see that there are two issues that lead directly to what is happening today, and they are a result of that break in communion and the events that followed.

Russia was primarily an Orthodox country, and the Russian Orthodox Church was established by the Patriarch of Constantinople at the request of the Russians (AD 988). The evangelization of Russia was, therefore, an Eastern evangelization. The Russian Orthodox Church grew to be the largest of the Orthodox Churches and eventually received autocephalous status (meaning that they were removed from the jurisdiction of the ecumenical patriarch) and the head of the Russian Church became a patriarch himself (1589). This church was not immune to the problems that plagued other churches, including their own reactionaries, revolutionaries, and heretics.

One of the problems that followed the Communist takeover of the country in 1917 was the underground movement of the church. But that was compounded by the placement of KGB agents within the church herself. Many became priests and a few became bishops. This caused no small concern on the part of the faithful. Further, Stalin suppressed (quite forcefully) the Ukrainian Catholics.

After the Union of Brest, Ukrainian Catholics had their own churches in Russia and other places under Communist control. All religions were suppressed by the government and their buildings confiscated. The churches were allowed to keep only those buildings used for worship. All religious education was suppressed, and all education—including the formation of priests—was turned over to the state. The only church with sufficient strength to offer any resistance was the Russian Orthodox Church, which, at the start of 1917 had reestablished the patriarchate (suppressed under Peter the Great in the eighteenth century) and elected the Metropolitan of Moscow, Tikhon, as the new patriarch but made him subject to the *sobor* (the synod of bishops).

Eventually, all "itinerant" preaching (preachers who did not have fixed churches) was prohibited. Catholics were not exempt from this, and found themselves persecuted severely. Eventually, only the Russian Orthodox Church was permitted to operate, and even there the state carefully supervised what was happening.

With the fall of communism (1989–1992), these Eastern Catholic Churches wanted their buildings back. Because all of the buildings and churches had been turned over to the state or to the Russian Church, this meant that someone would have to build a new church. The Russian Church did not want to undertake this since money was not available for this project.

In addition to this, there were issues of being a single church. Moscow is faced with several churches that claim to be "Orthodox," but that are not under the Patriarch of Moscow. In the mind of the patriarch, this confusion could lead to defections from the church in favor of Rome, *if* Rome were to undertake large-scale evangelization efforts. Moscow has, therefore, denied Rome access to the country (note, for example, that Pope John Paul II was never able to visit Russia, much to his dismay). In spite of this, Rome has appointed three bishops for territory within Russia.

The combination of these things have led to the problems between Rome and Moscow. However, as this book is being written, there are some indications of a thaw in relations between the two churches, which holds out some promise for future developments.

33. So, given everything you've said so far, why have the last thousand years been different from the first thousand years?

This is a question that goes beyond the scope of this book, but that also needs to be addressed, at least with a broad view.[7]

Let's begin by breaking the first thousand years into two five-hundred-year periods. During the first five hundred years, the church was growing and spreading throughout the Mediterranean world. It was also dealing with a series of heresies that threatened the unity of teaching. As a result, ecumenical councils were called to define the correct teaching.

The beginning of this period was also marked by persecutions under various Roman emperors. The influence of Rome was primarily that of arbiter *when asked* to fulfill that role. There was no legal (juridic) authority evidenced by Rome at this time. This was changing, however, as Pope Saint Leo I (the Great), who reigned from 440 to 461, *did* attempt to establish a juridic authority for the See of Rome over *all* churches. This effort was not continued after his death, but his efforts did, however, form the basis for future pontifical efforts to establish the primacy of Rome, not just of honor, but of authority as well.

During this first five hundred years there were periods of estrangement between East and West, but no serious disagreements that would sever the bonds of communion. Both East and West recognized their differences of expression in matters of theology and discipline, and determined that they were not of such significance that they were worth addressing.

This was not the case during the second five hundred years. East and West continued to drift apart, not so much in matters of practice, or even of theology, but in terms of the philosophical underpinnings of their theological expression and thought patterns. This divergence caused both sides to readdress issues that had previously been considered relatively minor. Among these were the use of leavened (Eastern practice) versus unleavened (Western practice) bread, married versus celibate clergy, and so on.

In the late second century, there was also the shift in the West from Greek as their common language to Latin. Tertullian (circa 160–220) was the first of the church fathers to write in Latin. Saint Augustine of Hippo (354–430) was a master of Latin and was part of the reason for the increased use of Latin in the West. However, the East continued to use Greek as their primary language. With the West losing their desire to study and know Greek, an intellectual schism began to develop between the East and the West that, eventually, helped contribute to the Great Schism.

Once the break occurred (this took nearly *six centuries* to complete), further estrangement between East and West took place. Foremost among these was the issue of the *filioque* (the phrase "and the son"), which we discuss in Question 60. Issues over the form of bread, the question of priestly celibacy, and other issues continued to cause difficulties. Further, the Latin Church called additional ecumenical councils (fifteen). Under the auspices of papal infallibility, formally defined at the First Vatican Council (1869–1870), Rome also defined certain matters of faith: the Assumption of Mary (November 1, 1950) and the Immaculate Conception (December 8, 1854), which are expressed in ways that make them difficult for the Orthodox to accept. Furtherance of the issue of papal supremacy has also complicated matters.

As a result, the minor slights of the first thousand years have been magnified during the second thousand years. The lifting of the mutual excommunications by Patriarch Athenagoras I and Pope Paul VI (October 1967) started the process of easing those tensions, but the process has barely started, and much remains to be done (see Question 101 for more on this).

34. What effect did the Crusaders' sack of Constantinople in 1204 have on church relations?

This question is, in reality, the key to many of the challenges we face today in getting the East and West to reunite. For many Orthodox, any discussion of this historical event leads one quickly to the conclusion that the sack happened yesterday instead of eight hundred years ago!

Pope Innocent III directed the Fourth Crusade with a stated goal of freeing Jerusalem by way of Egypt. Venice agreed to transport the troops. Because of financial difficulties, the Crusade was diverted by the Venetians to the town of Zara in Dalmatia (today Zadar in Croatia). This town was, in effect, an independent community, but was recognized by the king of Hungary, Emeric, who had agreed to join the Crusade. The citizens of Zara, recognizing the threat, tried to turn the Crusaders away by proclaiming themselves to be Christian. However, the Crusaders ignored this and, after a short siege, took the city. Pope Innocent III then excommunicated the Crusaders and the Venetians.

Political intrigue and clerical urging led the Crusaders to Constantinople. They reluctantly went to attack the city. However, when they arrived they were greeted warmly, and aided in placing Alexius Angeleus on the throne as Alexius IV. Following some political infighting, Alexius IV was killed, and the Crusaders, angered by this action, sacked the city of Constantinople, stole valuable relics and virtually all of the valuable articles used for the celebration of the Divine Liturgy. This very un-Christian action was probably the most significant in sealing the separation between the East and the West.

THREE

THE WORKINGS OF THE CHURCH

Such gold the holy martyr Lawrence [the Deacon] preserved
for the Lord. For when the treasures of the Church were
demanded from him, he promised that he would show them.
On the following day he brought the poor together. When
asked where the treasures were which he had promised, he
pointed to the poor, saying: "These are the treasures of
the Church." And truly they were treasures, in whom
Christ lives, in whom there is faith in Him.
— Saint Ambrose, *On the Duties of the Clergy,* Book II,
Chapter XXVIII

35. Are the Eastern Churches "under" the pope?

The easy answer is yes—sort of. According to canon law, the pope has jurisdiction over all the churches.[8] How this jurisdiction is carried out depends on a number of factors. First, it depends on the structure of the church in question. Generally the pope works through his curia, and, for the Eastern Catholic Churches, this would be the Congregation for Oriental Churches. According to their profile, "This Dicastery received from the Supreme Pontiff the mandate to be in contact with the Oriental Catholic Churches for the sake of assisting their development, protecting their rights and also maintaining whole and entire in the one Catholic Church, alongside the liturgical, disciplinary and spiritual patrimony of the Latin Rite, the heritage of the various Oriental Christian traditions" (Vatican Web Site Dicastery Profile).

If the pope needs to work directly with a given church he will deal with the head of that church or, if there is no head, may act directly. The structure of the church determines if there is a head. Generally, patriarch and archepiscopal churches have a head, while other structures do not.

There is, however, a more appropriate understanding of this relationship. The Eastern Catholic Churches are "in communion" with the pope. This means that the pope recognizes the various Eastern Catholic Churches as valid churches and has entered into an agreement by which the sacraments/mysteries are shared between members of the various churches. This description more fully recognizes the fact that some of these churches have their own heads.

36. What do you mean by "head of the church"? I thought the pope was *the* head of the church?

Once again we have to distinguish between the various roles that the pope has. The pope is, first and foremost, the Bishop of

Rome. As such, he is the head of the church in Rome. He is also the Patriarch of the West and, therefore, the legal head of all Roman Catholic Churches (Latin Rite Churches). As the pope, he is responsible for maintaining unity in the church and, to that end, has legal jurisdiction over all the churches in communion with him.

However, in the theology of the church, *each* bishop, as a successor to the apostles, is the "head" of his own church or diocese (in the East these may be called "eparchies"). But different church structures exist that support a formal "head" of the church. For example, Patriarch Gregory III is the head of the Melkite Church; Patriarch Stephanos II is the head of the Catholic Coptic Church, and so on.

There are, however, some limitations on these patriarchs. For example, the Melkite patriarch has authority over the Liturgy that is served in any Melkite parish anywhere in the world. He has direct authority, however, only over the clergy and laity in the *territory* that is traditionally his (basically, the Middle East). So, the Melkite bishop of the United States (as of 2006, Archbishop Cyril Salim Bustros) had his appointment confirmed by the pope—after his predecessor, Bishop John Elya, submitted his resignation to the pope. Note that I said that Archbishop Cyril had his appointment *confirmed* by the pope. He was actually *elected* by the Melkite synod of bishops, but because the United States is not part of the Melkite patriarch's territory, the pope had to make the official appointment.

And, to be technically (and theologically) correct, Christ is the head of the church; the pope and the patriarchs are the *visible* heads of their respective churches.

37. What do you mean by "different church structures"?

Within the Eastern Catholic Churches the organization or "structure" of the church is quite variable. There are four types of church structures: patriarchal, major archepiscopal, metropolitan, and "other." There are also churches that have no hierarchy.

A patriarchal church is one headed by a patriarch. This includes the Chaldean, Armenian, Coptic, Syrian, Maronite, and Melkite Churches, all of whom have a patriarch. Like the pope, the patriarchs have a group of advisors. For the pope this is the College of Cardinals, while, for the patriarchs, it is their synod of bishops. A patriarch is elected by his own church, and his election is *not* confirmed by the Pope.[9] However, the man so elected must notify Rome of his election and is, in turn, recognized by Rome with the reception of the *pallium,* a wool "scarf" containing five crosses representing the wounds of Christ. Note that if no one is elected within fifteen days of the opening of the synod, the matter is to be referred to the pope.[10]

Major archepiscopal churches are those headed by a major archbishop. This includes the Romanian, Ukrainian, Syro-Malabar, and Syro-Malankara Churches. In these churches the major archbishop functions much like a patriarch, but does not have that title. In precedence they rank after patriarchal churches, and a major archbishop ranks behind a patriarch. A major archbishop is elected by his church, and his election *must* be confirmed by the pope.[11]

Metropolitan churches (technically, metropolitan *sui iuris*) are those churches that have bishops (called the "metropolitan bishop") as their heads. This bishop is *appointed* by Rome, assisted by the council of hierarchs of that church, usually from a list of three candidates submitted by the synod of bishops. These churches are established, modified, suppressed, and have their territorial boundaries defined by the pope, who may delegate this to the Congregation for Oriental Churches. Metropolitan churches include the Ethiopian and American Ruthenian Churches.

Finally, there are other Eastern Churches that are simply called "churches *sui iuris*" and that have either no specific head or, in fact, have no hierarchy (that is, no bishops) at all. The first group includes the Bulgarian, Greek, Hungarian, Italo-Albanian (sometimes called "Italo-Greek"), and the Slovak Churches. Churches with no hierarchy include the Belarusian, Albanian, Georgian, and

Russian Eastern Catholic Churches. These churches are all dependent upon Rome or, in practice, upon the local Latin Rite bishop.

38. Can a Roman Catholic (or Latin Catholic) go to Mass at any of these churches, and will it meet the Sunday obligation?

The simple answer is yes, they may go and, yes, it will satisfy the Sunday obligation. But the issue of obligation is an area in which East and West differ. For Eastern Catholics, the concept of an "obligation" to worship God does not exist any more than there is an obligation to breathe. If one does not breathe or eat one dies—this is not an obligation but, rather, a requirement of living. It is in this fashion that Eastern Catholics address worshiping God.

In the Eastern approach to Liturgy we recognize that *Christ* is the celebrant of the Liturgy and that all of us—bishop, priest, deacon, or layperson—*serve* the liturgy. We serve because of our baptism, which joins us to the royal priesthood. The role of each may be different, but together we form a "chorus" to sing the praises of God. In fact, Eastern liturgies are all sung!

As we pointed out in Question 5, the term *Mass* is used only by the Latin Church and the Syriac Churches. Generally, a better term that is used by all churches is *Liturgy,* although this encompasses more than just the Divine Liturgy, Quorbono, or Mass (for example, it includes the Liturgy of the Hours).

39. What is a patriarch?

A patriarch is a bishop chosen to lead a particular church. In rank he is just below the pope and above the cardinals. He is a bishop or, if not a bishop at the time of his election, must be ordained a bishop. He functions in much the same way as the pope does (in fact, the pope is also called "the Patriarch of the West").

One of the developments of the early church was the "pentarchy" or five patriarchies: Rome, Constantinople, Alexandria, Antioch, and Jerusalem. These were the major Sees of the church with, of course, the "primacy of honor" granted to Rome.

Today in the Catholic Church the patriarchs are the Patriarch of the West, the Pope of Rome, the Armenian Patriarch, the Coptic Patriarch (technically the Patriarch of Alexandria), the Maronite Patriarch (Antioch), the Melkite Patriarch (also Antioch), and the Syrian Church (also Antioch). For completeness sake, we should also note that the Antiochian Orthodox Patriarch and the Syrian Orthodox Patriarch also claim Antioch. So, this city where the followers of Christ were first called "Christians" has no less than *five* patriarchs!

While we're on this topic, we should also note that there are some honorific patriarchal Sees. The first of these was set up by the Crusaders in Jerusalem. The bishop who heads that diocese has the honorary title of Patriarch of Jerusalem. He is, of course, not a patriarch, because no patriarch can be under another patriarch's authority, and the pope is the Patriarch of the West. This is why, in Question 35, we qualified the understanding of the Eastern patriarchs being "under" the pope. They are in communion with him and, by virtue of that communion, grant him certain juridic power over them.

Other minor or honorary patriarchates include Venice (which is, itself, a combination of two honorary patriarchates, Aquileia and Grado) and Lisbon. Technically, there is still an honorary patriarch of Constantinople, Antioch, West Indies, and East Indies, although no one is assigned to these titular patriarchates.

40. What are the clerical ranks in the Eastern Churches?

The ranks of bishop, priest, and deacon are found in *all* Catholic Churches, whether Eastern or Latin. The Eastern Churches have, however, retained the minor orders, especially the subdiaconate, which, for many, is a permanent order—they do not progress to the diaconate or the priesthood.

As an historical note, these minor orders were porter, lector, exorcist, and acolyte. The major orders were subdeacon, deacon, and priest. Following Pope Paul VI's directive (in the *moto proprio*

Ministeria Quaedam, August 15, 1972), the minor orders and the major order of subdiaconate were suppressed in the Latin Church. The ministries of lector and acolyte were created, and the major orders were redefined as deacon, priest, and bishop. A man enters these ministries not by ordination, but by installation.

In general, the next "grade" of cleric is the reader, which exists in all Eastern Catholic Churches. There is no equivalent to porter or exorcist, and the functions of the Latin Church's acolyte are mostly done by the subdeacon in the Eastern Churches.

Entrance into the clerical state takes place with *tonsure,* that is, the cutting of some hair by the bishop.

41. The pastor of the Melkite Church near me is an archimandrite—what is that?

The title of Archimandrite is an honorary title that is granted to a priest who exercises authority over a monastery but, in recent years, has been granted in much the same way as the Latin Church uses the title of Monsignor. That is, it is given in recognition of exemplary service to the church. In the Byzantine tradition, the archimandrite is recognized by the use of the monastic veil. Note that the title of Hegumen is used more commonly to represent one who has authority over a monastery. In the West, an abbot is the head of a monastery or abbey.

42. What other titles do Eastern Catholic priests receive?

This is a complex question. If we begin with the Byzantine tradition, the honorific titles are Stavrophore (cross-bearing), Archimandrite (see Question 41), and, on very rare occasions, Exarch. Some jurisdictions also have the title Archpriest and even Mitered Archpriest (this latter has the right to wear a miter just like that worn by a bishop).

For the sake of completeness, the title of Stavrophore also refers to one of the three monastic grades that are granted to monks who are *not* priests. The other two grades are Rassophore (the first level after a novice formally enters into the monastic life) and Great Schema (the highest-level monk).

The Chaldean, Maronite, and Syrian Churches grant the title of Chorbishop to select priests who then function in a limited fashion as bishops. A chorbishop will wear the insignia of a bishop and may be called "Bishop" or "Father."

Although the question was about *priests,* there are also special titles that Eastern Catholic *deacons* may receive. These are, specifically, Archdeacon and Protodeacon. Technically, an archdeacon is a monastic while a protodeacon is simply one belonging to the secular or diocesan clergy.

43. Who appoints Eastern Catholic bishops?

This depends on the structure of the church. In patriarchal churches the synod of bishops in communion with the patriarch selects their own bishops from a list of candidates approved by Rome. Should a man not on that list be elected, his name must be sent to Rome for confirmation. In all other cases, a list of suitable candidates is sent to Rome, and the pope selects the bishop just as he does with the Latin Church.

On a separate but related note, *only* the pope can establish or remove a diocese or eparchy. So, in this sense, the Eastern Churches are as dependent upon the pope as is the Latin Church.

44. Do Eastern Catholics have cardinals? Do they have monsignors?

Yes.

Okay, that was probably not a very informative answer! The fuller answer is that there are some Eastern Catholic Churches that have clergy with these titles. The title of Monsignor is not an Eastern title and, in general, is no longer given in the Byzantine tradition, although it seems to be fully integrated into the Maronite Church. There are, at the time of writing this book, three Eastern Catholic cardinals. The Maronite Patriarch is a cardinal, the head of the Congregation for Eastern Churches is a cardinal, and the head of the Ukrainian Church is a cardinal. The cardinals vote in conclave to elect a pope.

45. Do Eastern Catholic Churches have religious orders like the Roman Catholic Church? What about nuns and religious brothers?

The religious orders of the Eastern Catholic Churches are quite different from those of the West. There are nuns and brothers—but they are usually found only in monasteries. For example, Holy Resurrection Monastery in the Mohave Desert of Southern California includes a number of monks who are not priests. Those who are fully professed are called "Father," while the others are called "Brother." As in the West, nuns are called "Sister."

Catholic religious orders in the East follow the rules of Saint Basil and, consequently, call themselves "Basilians." To take this a little further, there are two major Basilian orders in the Melkite Church: the Salvatorians and the Shuwerites. While both are monastics, there are such significant differences that they might as well be totally different orders.

Most Eastern religious are monastics and, consequently, are not often seen in parishes or schools, as is typical of Latin Catholic religious orders. Unlike many Orthodox monks, Eastern Catholic monks may be seen in activities outside their monasteries.

46. How are priests and deacons assigned to parishes in Eastern Churches? How often are they transferred?

In general, the assignment of priests and deacons functions much like the process in the Latin Church. The bishop examines the needs of the parishes and assigns priests who can meet those needs. Deacons who are going on to the priesthood are generally assigned in the same fashion, but only for a time. Permanent deacons usually are assigned based upon where they live and are, in general, not transferred unless they move or ask to be transferred.

There is no general answer for how long a priest may be at his assignment. Most of the Eastern Catholic Churches do not have such an exceptional number of priests that they can rotate men at will. Most parishes tend to be one-priest parishes, and thus clerics serve for long periods of time to allow them to develop some continuity in their programs and in the development of the spiritual and parish life of their communities.

47. What ever happened to the principle of "one city, one bishop"?

The principle of "one city, one bishop" worked well when there was less movement of people. That is, in the past, multiple generations of a family tended to be born, marry, have children, and die all in the same place. Since bishops have geographic limits, this worked well. However, as the migration of people from place to place became more pronounced, the principle began to be more difficult to enforce.

People wanted to keep their own traditions and forms of worship, and this was difficult if the form they were used to was not available. Then they would either adapt to what was present, or ask for priests who knew how to serve them. Here in the United States we experienced this in the growth of the national churches for the Germans, the Poles, the Italians, and the Irish, especially on the east coast and in Chicago. Each nationality brought its own priests. This wasn't a problem because all were of the Latin Rite.

Things became complicated when people from Eastern Churches moved into a mostly Latin area. Often the Latin bishop was asked to support the Eastern traditions. In some cases this worked well; in others it was a disaster. In the latter case, the people asked their bishops "back home" to send priests and, eventually, asked for their own bishops.

When bishops were sent or appointed, the "one city, one bishop" concept was fully obviated. It was no longer possible to support a single city with a single bishop, and overlapping territories appeared. For example, the Melkite bishop of the United States has jurisdiction over all fifty states! Clearly his territory overlaps that of many Latin Rite bishops, but it happens to also overlap that of two Maronite bishops (the Eparchy of New York and the Eparchy of Los Angeles), and so on.

FOUR

THEOLOGY

The theology of the early church interpreted the great Mystery
of godliness in terms which, if short of the fullness of the
Pauline conception, are yet so free from arbitrary assumptions,
so true to human nature as the wisest of men know it, so
true to the worthiest and grandest ideas of God.
— Saint Athanasius, *Treatise on the Incarnation of the Word,*
Introduction

48. What is the *filioque* and why is it an issue between East and West?

This question requires a three-part answer. First we'll address the meaning of the *filioque,* then the theology behind the *filioque,* and finally we'll address the "political" issues surrounding it.

First, the Latin word *filioque* simply means "and the son" (Latin *filius* means "son" and the *-que* ending means "and"). This word was added to the Nicene Creed in Spain in 587 (at the Council of Toledo, a local council) to counter a heresy called "Arianism."

Second, the goal theologically was to make sure that the people understood that not only were the Father and the Son *consubstantial*—meaning "of the same substance"—but that the Holy Spirit was also of that same substance. The result was that instead of reading, "And in the Holy Spirit, the Lord, the giver of life, who proceeds from the Father...," it now read, "And in the Holy Spirit, the Lord, the giver of life, who proceeds from the Father and the Son...." This seems to indicate that the Father is no longer the sole source of divine life because the Holy Spirit proceeds from *both* the Father *and* the Son. Theologians had to explain this. The result was the theological statement that the Son was "generated" by the Father and the Holy Spirit was "spirated" by the Father and the Son. Another explanation is that the Son is the "Word" thought by the Father and the Holy Spirit is the bond of love between Father and Son. Both these explanations have been understood by the Orthodox as an indication that the Father alone did not produce the Son and the Holy Spirit.

A more recent theological explanation used in dialogue with the Orthodox has attempted to provide a more scripturally sound understanding. Here the theologians postulate that the Holy Spirit is spirated from the Father *through* the Son. This is based upon John 15:26, where we read, "When the Advocate comes, whom I will send to you from the Father, the Spirit of truth who comes from the Father, he will testify on my behalf." Here the sense is clear that the Son *sends* the Holy Spirit—but that the Holy Spirit *comes from* the Father.

Last, there are three major political issues that need to be understood (and the term *political* here does not mean to mitigate the severity of the issues at hand): (1) the history of why this action was taken; (2) the fact that this phrase was unilaterally inserted into the Creed; and (3) the implications of this action on the universality of the church.

During the fourth century, a priest named Arius began to teach that the Son, Jesus, was *not* of the same substance as the Father and that there was a time when the Son did *not* exist. This was countered by the teaching of the First Council of Nicaea (325) in which the church fathers asserted that the Father and the Son *were* of the same substance (in Greek, *homoousios,* literally, "same substance"). The primary statement of this was the Nicene Creed. This didn't end the controversy, however. Some bishops thought that the term should be *homoiousios,* meaning "of *like* substance." The First Council of Constantinople (381) again attempted to resolve the argument. This resulted in a slight change to the Creed (officially now the Nicene-Constantinopolitan Creed). The reason for bringing all this up is to show that the Creed *could* be changed, but only by the *Universal* Church in *ecumenical* council.

But these two councils did not end the problem. A convert to Arian Christianity named Ulfilas (311–380/381) spread the message of Arianism to the Germanic regions of Europe. By the time the German people entered into the Roman Empire, they had a full century of training and education in the Arian form of Christianity. Clearly, the result was a conflict between the orthodox teachings of the empire and the heretical teachings the Germanic peoples were following. One consequence of this conflict was that Arianism spread to Spain. It was there that the

Council of Toledo made the decision to change the Creed by inserting the word *filioque* in 587.

From Spain the modified Creed spread to the Frankish lands. It was embraced by Charlemagne (Charles I, the King of the Franks) in 794. Pope Leo III (795–816) decreed that the modified Creed was not to be used, and had the Nicene-Constantinopolitan Creed inscribed in Latin and Greek on tablets in St. Peter's. His order, however, was not effective in the land of the Franks, who continued to use the modified Creed. Eventually (1014) the modified Creed was used in Rome. It is, today, the Creed used by *all* Latin Rite Catholics (although the pope does not use it when praying with Eastern Catholics).

Because the *filioque* was inserted by a synod or local council, the Eastern Churches simply thought it would go away. When that failed to happen, they rejected it, since they believed that any change to the Creed, which is a statement of the Universal Church, should come from the Universal Church in ecumenical council.

For more on this very interesting topic, one can read on the USCCB Web site the statement entitled, *The* Filioque: *A Church Dividing Issue? An Agreed Statement of the North American Orthodox-Catholic Theological Consultation.* This document provides a great deal of history and the theology behind the issue, far beyond what we've gone into here.

49. I've heard the terms *Great Lent* and *Presanctified*—what do they mean?

For Eastern Catholics (and Orthodox), there are several periods of fasting during the year. These are all generically referred to as "Lent" in the various writings. For example, we have the "Nativity Fast," which precedes the Nativity of the Lord (Christmas); the "Dormition Fast," which precedes the Feast of the Dormition of Mary (celebrated as the Assumption of Mary in the Latin Church); and the "Apostles' Fast," which takes place before the Feast of Peter and Paul on June 29. These are "little Lents," while Great Lent corresponds (approximately) to the period of Lent in the Latin Church. The reason I say "approximately" is that Lent starts differently for the Eastern Catholic Churches. For the Maronite Church, it starts with Ash Monday, which is the Monday before the Latin Church's Ash Wednesday. While Byzantine Churches don't use the name "Ash Monday" nor, in fact, do they have a custom of ashes, Great Lent does start on the Monday before what is called "Ash Wednesday" in the Latin Church.

The Maronite Church also has the same fasts, which they call Great Lent, Apostle's Lent (June 25 to June 28), Assumption Lent (August 7 to August 14), and Christmas Lent (December 13 to December 24).

We can now fit the Liturgy of the Presanctified into place. Because Great Lent is a time of penitence and not a time of rejoicing, the celebration of the Divine Liturgy is restricted to Sundays. During the week, priests celebrate the Liturgy of the Presanctified, usually only on Wednesday evening. This is much like what happens in the Latin Church with a communion service, or on Good Friday without the veneration of the cross. That is, there is no consecration, no confection of the Eucharist—the believers consume the Eucharist that was consecrated on the previous Sunday. What is unique about the Eastern approach to this is that there is a part of the loaf of bread called the "Lamb," which represents Christ. On the Sunday before we celebrate the Presanctified, the priest must consecrate two Lambs, one for that Sunday and one for the Presanctified. The Lamb is broken and placed into the chalice while the priest says, "Broken and distributed is the Lamb of God, broken and not dismembered, always eaten and never expended, but making holy those who receive it." The wine that is received at the Presanctified Liturgy is *not* consecrated, that is, it is not the Precious Blood of Christ. There is a presanctified liturgy found in all the Catholic Rites. For the Latin Rite the primary "presanctified" liturgy is that of Good Friday. Other occasions are when a communion service is used because no priest is available.

50. What is *theosis?*

Both the Latin Church and the Eastern Catholic Churches feature this idea as a central point in their theology. What is called "theosis" in the East is called "divinization" in the West. It is the process of becoming more like God. Many of the church fathers speak this simple truth, which is commonly attributed to Saint Athanasius (and to other church fathers such as Saint Augustine): "God became man that man might become God." Note that we do not become "a god" but, rather, are incorporated into the One God.

This is, as Saint Peter tells us, "partake[ing] of the divine nature."[12] *Theosis* is that process by which we strip away all that is not of God. We do not give up our selves, for that is a precious gift from God. We are, however, to find the true self in service to God and his people and, thereby, to grow in knowledge and love of God.

The Greek word *metanoia* is frequently associated with *theosis*. The word means "a conversion, a change of heart." Saint Paul speaks of conversion as a turning away from something *and* a turning toward something else. This is precisely the concept of metanoia, and it is the idea behind *theosis*. We turn from the things of this world—especially from sin—and turn *toward* God. By participating in the mysteries (sacraments) we are nourished and helped along this path so that, when we finally "fall asleep in the Lord" (in general, Eastern Catholics don't say "die" because we don't cease to exist, which is what that term implies), we are so much like God that we are welcomed into his presence. We say more about the idea of Purgatory in Question 62.

51. What are the fasting and abstinence practices of the Eastern Catholic Churches?

As we noted in Question 49, the Eastern Catholic Churches have more "Lenten" periods of fast than does the Latin Church. In addition, *all* Wednesdays and Fridays are days of abstinence (no meat). There are different traditions with regard to fasting among the different churches. First and foremost is that the guidelines for fasting are just that: guidelines! They are *not* designed to be followed explicitly and completely by everyone but, rather, they suggest what could be done. Eastern Catholics are expected to follow the directions given by their spiritual father (usually a priest or deacon in their parish, but it may be any learned and holy person).

Because the fasting practices are guidelines, there are two general approaches: a full fast and a modified fast. Abstinence means that we abstain from all meat (including fish), dairy products (milk, cheese, butter), eggs, wine (really, any alcoholic beverage), and even olive oil. The fasting requirement is that one does not eat solid food from midnight to noon. The law on fasting says that the first day of Great Lent is a day of fast and abstinence, all Fridays of Great Lent we abstain from meat, and Good Friday is a day of fast and abstinence. Many Eastern Catholics, however, follow a more rigid program that treats every day of Great Lent as a day of fast and abstinence, although Saturday, Sunday, and certain holy days are days when there is no fasting, and fish, wine, and olive oil are permitted. There are other compromises that may be made in discussion with one's spiritual father.

Sometimes the question comes up about whether or not it's a mortal sin if the fast is broken. Because these are guidelines and not hard and fast rules, the issue of mortal sin doesn't enter into the picture. In fact, depending on why the fast was broken, even venial sin may not apply. This is also a good place to point out that the differentiation between mortal sin and venial sin really doesn't exist in the East. Rather, all sin is seen as mortal, since all sin is offensive to God. For this reason, the East encourages confession before going to communion—even it that means weekly confession!

52. Are Eastern Catholic teachings the same as the Latin Catholic teachings?

The teachings are the same in nearly every instance. There are theological *expressions* that differ, usually because there is a different theological approach in the East than is found in the

West. Among the more notable differences are the theology of marriage; the understanding of Mary, the Mother of God (or, as she is called in the East, the "Theotokos"); the understanding of original sin, Purgatory, and so on. There are also differences in practices between the Latin and the Eastern Churches.

Since we touch on original sin, the Immaculate Conception, and Purgatory later (see Questions 60–62), we'll leave those for now and, for an example, will look at the theology of marriage (see also Question 84). This sacrament, called the "Mystery of Holy Crowning" in the Byzantine tradition, and the "sacrament of holy matrimony" in the Coptic and Latin Churches (the Coptic understanding is that *sacrament* is an unseen gift from God while *mystery* means obscurity). For Eastern Catholics the general understanding is that death does not terminate or end a marriage. One may remarry after the death of a spouse, but such a marriage is always seen as an aid and comfort to the one left behind, and should not be celebrated with the same joy and public display as was the case with the first marriage.

A second difference is found in the minister of this sacrament/mystery. For Latin Rite Catholics, the couple *themselves* are the ministers of the sacrament. This is why only a marriage between two baptized persons can be considered a sacrament; if one party is not baptized, that person cannot confer the sacrament on the other, nor can that person receive the sacrament! For Eastern Catholics, however, the priest or bishop is the minister of the sacrament. Thus, *only* a priest or bishop may marry a couple in the Eastern Churches, while, for the Latin Church, the bishop, priest, or deacon serves as the "official witness" for the church of the exchange of vows.

This brings us to a third difference. In the Byzantine tradition, there is no exchange of vows. The couple's very presence and the actions they take speak of their desire to enter into the marriage. In those countries where an exchange of vows is required, the churches add the vows, usually before the ceremony, simply for the sake of the civil proprieties.

In an Eastern Catholic marriage, the most common feature is the crowning of the couple. They are crowned for two reasons: first to show that they are the king and queen in their home and, second, to show that they are to be martyrs for their family. Martyrs are said to have "earned the crown of martyrdom," and this idea is carried over into the marriage ceremony. In the Coptic tradition, the groom is vested in a chasuble to show that he is the "priest" in the family.

53. What do you mean when you say in Question 52 that Eastern Catholics use a "different theological approach"?

The Latin Rite Church developed a philosophy and approach to theology that is called "kataphatic." This approach attempts to reveal and define what can be known of God and his actions among us. Scholasticism, the approach of Saint Thomas Aquinas (1225 or 1227–1274), is the fullest flowering of this approach. If one reads Saint Thomas Aquinas's finest work, the *Summa Theologica,* one finds an attempt to rationalize, to explain the fullness of the theology of the Latin Church. Examples of this are found in the terms we use for God: he is Almighty, Omniscient, Omnipresent, and so on. These are positive terms that describe what God is.

The East, however, uses an "apophatic" approach. That is, God is not defined (since one cannot circumscribe God with definitions) but, rather, what *is not* God is defined. So God is described as unknowable, uncontainable, untouchable, and unapproachable. These terms are not meant as absolutes because, clearly, we can know something of God through his revelation of himself, we can approach him in prayer and the mysteries, we can speak of the womb of the Theotokos (Mary the Mother of God) as "containing the uncontainable." But these terms indicate the lack of knowledge that we must always have with regard to God.

But this approach goes far beyond how we see God. It is found in all aspects of our theological expression. Rather than attempt to define the reality of the mysteries, what brings them into being and how they affect us, the East simply says that the mysteries *do* exist, and that they *are* beneficial to our spiritual lives.

54. Are the saints in the East different from those in the West?

The technical answer is no, they are not. When the Eastern Catholic Churches came into communion with Rome they brought their saints, and those saints became Western saints, if they were not already saints in the West. Now, having said that, the reality is that the East tends to honor those saints that were part of the East while the West continues to honor the saints of the West. Many, of course, are *both* Eastern and Western saints. Among the more prominent Eastern saints are Saint Basil, Saint Gregory of Nyssa, Saint Gregory the Theologian, Saint Athanasius, Saint John Chrysostom, and Saint John Damascene). Among the Western saints that are prominent in the East are Pope Saint Leo the Great and Pope Saint Gregory the Great. And, of course, both East and West celebrate the famous Eastern saint Nicholas of Myra! There are also saints that people in the West may not have heard of, such as Saint Gregory Palamas, whose writings give us an understanding of hesychasm, a form of spirituality commonly found in Eastern monasteries.

55. Does the pope name the saints for the Eastern Catholic Churches?

A "universal saint" is named by the pope. However, a given church may have a popular devotion to a saint who has not been proclaimed by the Universal Church. In this case, we have a "local saint." One such saint would be the Maronite, Saint Charbel, who was beatified by Pope Paul VI in 1965 and canonized by Pope Paul II in 1977. He had been revered by the Maronites as a saint, and they brought his case to Rome for universal devotion. There were also local saints who were venerated in a particular region. This has always been the case in the church, however, and should not be seen as something new or unusual.

In the early days of the Universal Church, the declaration that someone was a saint was done by popular acclaim. That is, the people themselves chose who was and who wasn't a saint. This was usually done on the basis of a heroic life or a particularly strong witness to the faith. Such would be the case, for example, for the early popes. All of the early popes are saints, and all were proclaimed saints by popular acclamation because of their living example of faith.

We have an example currently in process. In the Melkite Church there was a young man named Fathi Baladi (1961–1980). His case is currently under review by the Holy Synod of the Melkite Church. Should they decide that he is, indeed, a saint, they can make such a proclamation. This would establish him as a saint as far as the Melkite Church is concerned. Should they wish to make him a universal saint, then the case would need to be submitted to Rome and the declaration made by the Holy Father.

56. Why don't the Eastern Churches have statues?

The biggest reason is that statues are not a part of the Eastern tradition. For the Eastern Catholic, the use of icons provides what statues provide in the West. Because the Eastern Catholic Churches developed in an area where statues were associated with pagan cults (which was also true in Rome), Eastern Catholics did not develop a sense that these three-dimensional representations were beneficial. Additionally, the East does not represent anything "perfectly"—that is, as it exists in nature. In Western theology it is said that grace perfects nature. This is why the statues represent things "perfectly." As you'll see in Question 57 on icons, this is not what is done in the East.

There was even a period in history, during the eighth century, when the use of statues or icons was prohibited by law. This was due to a heresy called "iconoclasm" in which the idea (still held by many Protestants) that any representation of God was prohibited by Scripture. As a result, many early icons (and statues) were destroyed.

57. What's the significance of icons?

Following up on the previous question, icons serve as "windows into heaven" for the Eastern Christian. They are painted (some would say "written") in one of several very specialized styles. There are multiple styles: Arabic, Greek, and Russian are the most common styles one sees in the United States, although there is also a Coptic style that differs from the Arabic style.

These icons may be used to represent events such as the finding of the true cross, the baptism of Jesus in the Jordan, or the resurrection. They may represent the saints. They may represent Jesus. They may *not* represent the Holy Spirit or the Father because we do not know what God looks like. Jesus took human form, and so he may be represented.

Icons serve a function that is similar to statues or paintings in the Latin Rite Churches—they are to remind us of certain events or people in order to help us to focus our lives and actions on becoming more and more like Christ in all things.

As we mentioned in Question 56, the heresy of iconoclasm developed in the eighth century. In 726, Emperor Leo III published an edict declaring all images to be idols, forbidden by Exodus 20:4–5.[13] Patriarch Germanus (715–730) wrote to the emperor and to Pope Gregory II (713–731) objecting to the edict. Leo removed Germanus from office and replaced him with Anastasius (730–754), who was an iconoclast and had been the syncellus (in the West he would be the bishop's secretary). Because the monks were great defenders of the use of icons, they were persecuted. The pope also supported the use of icons and refused to destroy the statues or icons used in the West. Leo ordered Gregory to call a general council to address this.

Following the death of Gregory II, the new pope, Gregory III, continued to defend the practice of using images. In a local synod of Rome (731), all those who had taken or broken images used in worship were excommunicated. In 787 the Second Council of Nicaea declared that the use of images in worship was not only *not* prohibited, but was beneficial.

58. Do Eastern Catholics have the same seven sacraments as Roman Catholics?

Yes. Most of the Eastern Catholic Churches use the term *mystery* where the Latin Church uses the term *sacrament*. The Eastern Churches generally accept as the primary sacraments the same seven sacraments as the West. However, the East sees any action of God working in us as a "sacrament" and so does not limit the count to seven.

Again, this is not too surprising. If one looks at the list of sacraments that the early church fathers recognized, one notices a number of things that, in the Latin Church, are called "sacramentals." In the East there is a distinction between the seven mysteries and all other ways that God sends us grace. The basic understanding of this flows from a common prayer in which we recognize that God is "present in all places and filling all things."

So, while the seven sacraments of the Latin Church are certainly the most highly regarded sacraments of the Eastern Church, and the only ones regularly called "sacraments," there are other ways in which the grace of God flows to believers, and these, too, may be called sacraments.

One example of these "non-sacrament" sacraments is the church herself! Recent statements from Rome, both in the documents of the Second Vatican Council[14] and in the *Catechism of the Catholic Church*,[15] have begun to reflect the long-standing view of the East that the church is, indeed, a sacrament. If we think back to the old *Baltimore Catechism,* which defined a *sacrament* as an "outward sign instituted by Christ to give grace," we find that certainly describes the church.

59. Why do Eastern Catholic babies get to go to communion?

Eastern Catholics wonder why Latin Catholic babies aren't allowed to receive communion! The East cannot understand why babies are baptized and then not allowed to receive another sacrament until they are seven years old—and then the sacrament they receive—reconciliation (first confession)—is not one of the "sacraments of initiation," which are baptism, confirmation/chrismation, and Eucharist.

Eastern Catholics approach this as did the early church (including the Latin Church) for most of the first eight centuries. This practice is seen in the Latin Church in the Rite of Christian Initiation of Adults (RCIA), in which the elect are baptized, confirmed, and then receive communion. The theology here is that baptism brings the Holy Spirit to dwell within us, conforms us to the death and resurrection of Jesus, and makes whole the image and likeness of God. Confirmation seals or completes that process and gives us our "marching orders." It is through confirmation that we receive our call, our mission in life. Finally, the Eucharist sets our feet on the path by nourishing us spiritually.

In the Latin Church there is a desire to bring knowledge to the person; the communicant must be able to distinguish between ordinary bread and the Eucharist. In the East this is made clear by *where* and *how* one receives the Eucharist. So the East doesn't see *knowledge* as a requirement for the reception of communion. Consequently, there is no reason an infant *can't* receive communion. After all, that child was baptized, confirmed, and made his or her first communion already!

60. I heard that the Eastern Catholics don't believe in original sin. Is that correct?

That is certainly not correct. Eastern Catholics do believe in original sin, although there is a slightly different understanding of it as well as a different way of expressing it.

The Latin Church's vision of original sin is that of Saint Augustine. He teaches that through the sin of Adam our relationship with God was broken, we lost original justice, but we also inherited the "stain" of Adam's sin. It is this stain that is washed away in baptism. Thus, the unbaptized cannot be in God's presence for they have the stain of sin on their souls. Further, Augustine speaks of "the bonds of inherited guilt."[16] Finally, of course, we recognize that death is the consequence of original sin. Later teachings in the Latin Rite tell us that we also have a weakening of the will and a lessening of the intellect as a result of original sin.

For the Eastern Catholic, original sin is seen not in terms of stain and guilt, but of the condition of the world into which we are born. The "stain" of the Latin Rite becomes the distortion of the image of God that is the inheritance of all who are created "in the image and likeness"[17] of God. The primary result of original sin, however, is death. Because of this sin, we are bound to die.

Of course, there is some common theology with regard to original sin. We are all made in the image and likeness of God, but that image is distorted because of original sin. In baptism the image is restored. But, because we still live in a world affected by original sin, we do not have the relationship with God that we are supposed to have, nor do we have the state of holiness that is also supposed to be present. Therefore, we spend a lifetime of theosis or, as it is called in the West, divinization, attempting to become more and more like God (see Question 50).

61. I was looking at the feast days for the local Eastern Catholic Church and noticed they don't celebrate the Immaculate Conception—isn't that required for all Catholics?

The Eastern Catholic Church believes in the Immaculate Conception, since, as part of being "in communion" with Rome, all dogmatic teachings of the church are accepted. However, holy days are a function of the particular church and are not universal (with a few exceptions). In this case, the Eastern Churches generally celebrate the Maternity of Anne (Mary's mother).

The reason for this is technical, but let's see if we can't provide a reasonable explanation that doesn't require a degree in philosophy! The teaching of the Latin Church is based upon the philosophy of the Scholastics, which, in turn, is based upon the philosophy of Aristotle. However, Eastern theology does not use this philosophy and, therefore, does not find that the teachings derived from this are consistent with the Eastern approach.

Since the Eastern understanding of original sin is different from that of the West, the basic premise of the Immaculate Conception makes no sense to the Orthodox East. Since we are *all* born without original sin (remember, it's the state of the world into which we are born), it follows that this teaching on Mary is not quite the same in the East. However, the understanding of the West is that Mary was without sin from the moment of her *conception,* while the Eastern understanding is that Mary was "ever sinless." This may sound like it is the same thing, but it isn't. Rather, the Eastern view is that Mary may have been affected by original sin since that is the condition of the world. And, rather than think this is only an Eastern view, we need to acknowledge that many theologians attempt to come to grips with the issue of Mary's sinlessness. Saint Thomas Aquinas, for example, held that Mary was "first conceived in the flesh, and afterwards sanctified in the spirit."[18] Of course, this was before the Latin Church formally introduced the teaching of the Immaculate Conception. That teaching finds its basis in the theology of "anticipatory redemption" found in the work of John Duns Scotus and William of Ware.

Eastern teachings on Mary may have an even greater emphasis on Mary than the West. For Eastern Catholics she is the Theotokos (Mother of God). She is "higher than the Seraphim, more glorious than the Cherubim."[19] Her icon is always to the left of the holy doors as one faces the *iconostasis* (literally "icon stand," but, in the Byzantine tradition, the "wall" that separates the "holy place" or sanctuary from the main body of the church, upon which are placed icons). In the litanies chanted at the Divine Liturgy we find this: "Let us remember our all-holy, spotless, most highly blessed and glorious Lady the Theotokos and ever-virgin Mary."[20]

62. In a discussion with an Orthodox coworker, he said his church doesn't teach about Purgatory. What do Eastern Catholics teach with regard to this?

Once again we come to an issue of different philosophies. Eastern Catholics, who do accept all dogmatic teachings of the Latin Church—accept the *concept* of Purgatory, but explain it a little differently. In fact, the most current teachings from Rome are, again, more in line with the Eastern thinking.

For Eastern Catholics, there is an understanding that there is a purgation of all that would separate us from God. How this takes place is not defined (remember, the East tends not to define things to the degree that the West does). There have been a number of attempts at explaining this, both on the part of the Eastern Catholics and the Orthodox as well.

In the end, however, the East simply says that those who will be admitted to God's presence will be purged of what remains of their sinfulness.

63. Do Eastern Catholics believe in transubstantiation?

The term *transubstantiation* is not used in Eastern theology. In order to put this into perspective, however, we need to make sure we are all on the same page.

The teaching on the Eucharist dealing with the Real Presence is clear and concise in both the East and the West. That is, *Jesus is present* under the *forms* of bread and wine. The West, using the philosophy of Aristotle, went further and talks about "accidents" and "substance" in order to explain what happens at the consecration. The term *accidents* refers to the properties of a thing that are perceivable: height, weight, color, scent, thickness, taste, and so on. The term *substance* refers to the "thing-ness" of something. That is, a rose is a rose not because of its color, scent, or appearance, but because it has the substance of a rose and, consequently, the accidents (color, scent, appearance) are present because they go along with the substance.

In the case of the Eucharist, the bread and wine before the consecration have both the substance of bread or wine *and* the accidents of bread or wine. There are two changes that take place during the consecration: the bread and wine cease to exist as bread and wine because the substance of bread and wine become the substance of Jesus, and the accidents of bread and wine remain without their substance. So, for the West, the change of substance is called "transubstantiation."

For the East, however, the philosophy of Aristotle does not enter the picture. It is simply acknowledged that the bread and wine are no longer bread and wine but are really the body and blood of Jesus. This is clearly expressed in the prayer before communion said by both the clergy and the laity:

> I believe, Lord, and profess that You are the Christ, the Son of the Living God, come to this world to save sinners, of whom I am the greatest. I believe also that this is really your spotless body and that this is really your precious blood. Wherefore I pray to You: have mercy on me and pardon my offenses, the deliberate and the indeliberate, those committed in word and in deed whether knowingly or inadvertently; and count me worthy to share without condemnation your spotless mysteries, for the remission of sins and for eternal life. Amen.[21]

So, while the East uses neither the term *transubstantiation* nor the philosophy that underlies it, there is certainly belief in the Real Presence, in the transformation of the bread and wine into the Body and Blood of Jesus.

64. How do Eastern Catholics reconcile their teachings with those of the Roman Catholic Church?

In general, there's nothing to reconcile since the faith is the same, and the same beliefs are held. What varies is in the expression of the faith and in the theological approach (see Question 52). There are differences in practices, different fasting requirements, different holy days, differences in understanding "obligation," but, for the most part, these are not theological differences.

One noticeable difference is in the minister of marriage: in the Latin Church, it's the couple, and, in the Eastern Churches, it's the priest. Rome has acknowledged this difference in the canons of the East and the West, so there is no reconciliation and no problem between the two approaches.

65. Do Eastern Catholic Churches use girl altar servers?

No. In the Eastern tradition only the ordained may go behind the iconostasis to serve the Liturgy. There are two exceptions to this. In parishes that don't have enough clergy, young men and adult men may be admitted to serve as altar servers. In this role they wear the *sticharion,* the robe common to all ranks of the clergy. The other exception is found in convents and monasteries where there are only women. In those cases some may be selected to serve as altar servers, but instead of wearing the sticharion, they wear their normal black habits.

66. Do Eastern Catholic Churches have extraordinary ministers of holy communion?

A couple of years ago the answer would have been no. There is discussion among some of the Eastern Catholic Churches that would permit the use of an extraordinary minister of holy communion to be used *if necessary.* In general the bishop, the priest, and, if needed, the deacon are the only ones to give out communion. Even the use of the deacon is "extraordinary" in some of the Eastern Catholic Churches.

67. Do Eastern Catholics use leavened or unleavened bread?

Both. Most Eastern Catholic Churches use leavened bread, while a few (such as the Maronites) use unleavened bread. In general, the more contact the church had with the Latin missionaries the more likely they are to use unleavened bread (which is, of course, the norm in the Latin Church). Leavened bread is used to represent the fact that Christ is the "yeast" that causes his people to "rise." Unleavened bread, of course represents the "bread of haste" from the story of the Exodus.

Although leavened bread is used, it is supposed to be made of wheat, water, and yeast only. Other materials are not to be added to the bread.

Interestingly, there is no use of low-gluten breads for those who suffer from Celiac disease. If a person is gluten intolerant, they may ask that the bishop, priest, or deacon giving communion give them only the Precious Blood.

68. Is it true that priests are the "ordinary ministers" of confirmation?

Yes. In the early church the bishop was the minister of the sacraments of initiation (baptism, confirmation/chrismation, and Eucharist), which were all celebrated at the same time.[22] Later, as the church grew, the bishop was not able to do this for everyone. In the West it became the function of the priest to baptize and give first communion, while confirmation was reserved to the bishop. This resulted in celebration of the sacraments being separated by significant periods of time. As a result of this separation, the sacrament of confirmation became a sacrament in search of a theology. Recently, various dioceses in the United States have begun the process of restoring the original order of baptism, confirmation/chrismation, and Eucharist rather than the current general practice of baptism, first confession, first communion, and then confirmation. This is also true for all who go through the Rite of Christian Initiation of Adults: they are baptized, confirmed, and make their first communion in a single ceremony. This Rite is for all who are seven years of age and older.

In the East, however, the bishops took a different approach. They permitted the priests to complete the baptism with confirmation and then to give first communion (usually, just some of the Precious Blood since the child is usually not old enough for solid food). Since confirmation/chrismation is given at the time of baptism, there is rarely a case where it is given separately, as was the case in the Latin Church. Consequently, the priest is, indeed, the ordinary minister of confirmation.

69. I noticed that Eastern Catholics make the sign of the cross differently. Why do they do that?

There are several theories about why Eastern Catholics and Latin Catholics make the sign of the cross differently. Both the Eastern priest or bishop and the Latin bishop, priest, or deacon sign the people starting at the top of the "cross" and moving down, then to the left and the right. Latin Catholics "copy" the direction of the blessing, so that when the minister giving the blessing moves to the left, the one receiving the blessing moves his or her hand to the left shoulder, and then to the right. The Eastern Catholic "mirrors" the action of the priest or bishop—that is, the first shoulder is the right shoulder, which is where the bishop or priest's hand would be when he moves left.

Of course, because the church likes to use analogy in explaining things, theologies were developed to explain where the hand went and why. For the Eastern Catholic, the Son sits at the "right hand of the Father," and, thus, when we refer to the Son in the sign of the cross we touch the right shoulder.[23] For the Latin Catholic, the idea is that the sheep are on the right and the goats on the left (compare Matt 25:31–46), and we've been moved, through the action of Christ, from the left to the right to be with the sheep.

All of this is mostly a matter of popular tradition. There is, however, a deep theology in the way the Eastern Catholic holds his or her hand when making the sign of the cross. The thumb, index, and middle fingers are held together to remind us of the Trinity, the ring and little finger are held together to remind us of the two natures of Christ: human and divine. Finally, those last two fingers are held down to the palm to remind us that Christ came down from heaven to bring salvation to the world.

70. While watching a Divine Liturgy on television, I noticed the priest and deacon bowing a lot. Why?

Bows, or as they are called in the East, *metanies,* are a sign of conversion. Generally there is a short prayer associated with each of these metanies. Before the Liturgy starts, the prayer is, "O God, be propitious to me a sinner and have mercy on me." At other times: "O Lord, you will open my lips and my mouth will proclaim your praise," or "Glory to God in the highest, on earth peace and good will to men."

These prayers, and the metanies, are reminders of our constant need for conversion and reconciliation with God.

71. Is there a pattern to the use of icons?

It depends on what you mean by "use of icons." If, by that, you are referring to the icons on the iconostasis (see Question 76 for a full explanation of the iconostasis), then, yes, there is a pattern. As you face the royal or holy doors in the middle of the iconostasis, the icon of Christ should be to the right of the doors and the icon of Mary to the left of the doors. To the right of Christ should be the icon of Saint John the Baptist and to the left of Mary should be the icon of the parish church. This would normally mean an icon of the patron saint of the parish. Obviously, if the parish is named after something other than a saint, then this icon may be of an event. For example, my Melkite parish is named "Holy Cross" and the icon is that of the finding of the holy cross. Usually the "deacon's doors" have an icon of a deacon saint on them (one of whom is usually Saint Stephen the Protomartyr). If there are other icons on the iconostasis, they may be of the parish's choosing—there's no fixed "rule" regarding them. The holy doors themselves contain icons of the Annunciation (usually Mary and the Angel Gabriel) as well as the four evangelists (Matthew, Mark, Luke, and John). Over the holy doors is an icon of the Mystical or Last Supper but usually representing only Christ, not the apostles.

The next rank or row usually contains the apostles or the special "festal icons," which represent the various feast days. Finally, at the top of the iconostasis is the cross. Note that these rules are not totally fixed in place. Again, my parish has the festal icons on the walls around the church, and they can be moved to the front during the appropriate time of the year.

72. I thought we weren't allowed to have blue vestments, yet I see Eastern Catholic clergy wearing blue. What about that?

The Eastern Church doesn't have any prohibition against using blue vestments. In fact, blue is probably the most commonly used color of all the vestments in the Eastern Catholic Churches that follow the Byzantine tradition. Even in the Latin Church blue may be worn in places that have a dispensation for it. One such place was Spain, where blue was worn on feasts of the Blessed Virgin.

73. Are the liturgical colors the same for the Eastern Churches as for the Western Church?

This question is tied in with the previous question. For the Eastern Catholic Churches of the Byzantine Rite, there really are no "liturgical colors." Rather, there are "light" and "dark" colors. The light colors are generally gold, white, blue, and green while the dark colors are violet/purple and red. Also, unlike the Latin Church, a priest or deacon may wear different colors at the same Liturgy.

As noted in Question 72, for the Byzantine Rite blue vestments are more common (just as green vestments are the most commonly worn in the Latin Church). Green is traditionally worn in the Byzantine Rite for Pentecost and may be worn during the season of Pentecost.

Other Eastern Catholic Churches also have a different approach to the concept of liturgical colors but, in general, do not have the same concept as the Latin Church. For example, the Chaldeans seem to favor either white/gold or red. So, in general, it's fair to say that there is no such thing as a "liturgical color" in the Eastern Catholic Churches.

74. Do Eastern Catholics have eucharistic adoration, exposition, and benediction?

The full answer is, no, these practices are not Eastern. These elements of Latin tradition grew out of the need for people to have a devotion that was accessible to them. As fewer and fewer Latin Rite Catholics spoke and understood Latin, the Mass became less and less accessible to them (we have to remember that printed missals with Latin and its translation for the laity were not available until the twentieth century). Consequently, the people developed their own devotions.

Since the Eucharist was always reserved for the sick (and this is true in *both* the Latin Rite Church and in all Eastern Catholic Churches), the people developed their own devotion of spending time before the Blessed Sacrament in prayer. Eastern Catholics, however, tended to spend that time in the "icon corner" of their homes. This was an area where they had gathered particular icons, usually one of Christ, one of Mary, and then icons for the patron saints of the family members. They would also have a candle and, sometimes, a hand censer for incense.

Eucharistic benediction grew out of the Latin Church's desire to offer more to the people than simply spending time in prayer before the Blessed Sacrament. Benediction offered formal prayer and the blessing granted by the priest with the Blessed Sacrament. Today this blessing may be given by a bishop, priest, or deacon. Again, because the adoration of the Blessed Sacrament never developed in the Eastern Churches, the idea of benediction never arose.

Now, having said that, we also acknowledge that both of these practices *did* arise in the Eastern Catholic Churches in the United States, where, because of a number of factors beyond the scope of this book, numerous latinizations took place. Many Eastern parishes began to offer Latin devotions: eucharistic adoration, benediction, stations of the cross, and recitation of the rosary, for example. Following the Second Vatican Council, these were to have been eliminated, as the Eastern Churches were to return to practices that were authentically their own.[24]

Just as a point of interest, Eastern Churches of the Byzantine Rite *do* reserve the Blessed Sacrament for the sick on their altars in what's called an "artiphorion"—the Byzantine equivalent of a tabernacle. This is normally quite small, however, and contains only enough Eucharist for the sick.

But, in spite of all that has been said here, the *Byzantine Daily Worship* ritual book does, indeed, include a eucharistic benediction ritual because it was found in some Byzantine Churches as part of the latinizations that we've already mentioned.

75. I saw an Eastern Liturgy on television, and they were giving communion with a spoon. Why is that?

Communion in the Eastern Catholic Churches is always given by what's called "intinction." This means that the eucharistic bread (the term *host,* while common in the Latin Church, isn't used in the East) is mingled with the Precious Blood before being given to the communicant. Some Byzantine Churches, normally the Slavic

Churches, place the consecrated bread into the chalice before distribution. This necessitates the use of a spoon to give communion.

Melkites, however, do not do this, nor do the non–Byzantine Catholic Churches. Melkites cut the *prosphora* (the bread used for communion) into longer strips that are then dipped into the Precious Blood for each communicant. This method is also used by the other Eastern Catholic Churches, even those that use a host like that found in the Latin Rite Church.

As usual, there is an exception for the Melkites. When they celebrate the Presanctified Liturgy (see Question 49), they use the spoon for communion, for the same reason that the Slavic Byzantine Churches do—the reserved Blessed Sacrament has been mixed with wine (not the Precious Blood).

76. Why is there a wall in some Eastern Churches between the people and the altar?

Ah, you must be referring to the iconostasis (mentioned in Questions 61, 65, and 71), which is found in Byzantine and Coptic Churches. It is not found in other Eastern Catholic Churches. While the development of the iconostasis as it is known today is fairly well defined, the origin of a barrier between the people and the "holy place" is not at all well defined. The earliest form of the iconostasis seems to have been simply columns on which were placed icons of Jesus, Mary, and various saints. There was also, in the early churches, a low fence similar to the altar rail of the Latin Church.

Following the defeat of the iconoclasts in 787, the Byzantine Churches began a process of putting up more and more icons. At first this was done using stands (which are, themselves, called "the iconostasis"). Later, the use of a wall to hold the icons developed. Most likely this took place first in Byzantium, where the influence of the government led to the use of the "royal doors" (the term *royal* refers to both the emperor and the King of Kings).

In the Latin Church the closest we come to this would be the use of the "rood screen" in England, although this was normally not as high as the icon screen. In terms of the purpose and function of the iconostasis, some claim that the *reredos* of the Latin Church (the decorative wall behind the altar) is equivalent. While it is certainly true that both were used to enhance the beauty of the altar, there are significant differences in the theology around them.

The icons themselves are seen as "windows into heaven" and point out the fact that, in the Liturgy, heaven and earth touch. The area behind the iconostasis, the "holy place," represents heaven, while the nave of the church represents earth. The deacon, going back and forth, actually represents both Christ in his ministry of service and the angels who carry messages to the throne.

So, the best answer would be that the reason for the iconostasis is not to prevent people from seeing what is happening at the altar, but rather to indicate that we are, indeed, in the place where heaven and earth touch, where God in all his glory resides in the form of bread and wine.

77. I recently attended a wedding at an Eastern Catholic Church. Why didn't I see any stations of the cross?

You may recall that in Question 74 we talked about "latinizations"—that is, the introduction of Latin practices into the Eastern Catholic Churches. The stations of the cross are a development that happened in the West (probably during the twelfth century, but no earlier than the eleventh) but not in the East. Consequently, there are no stations of the cross in *most* Eastern Catholic Churches. As with other practices, they may have crept into use in some Eastern parishes, but should now be phased out.

But I suspect the answer to this question needs to have some additional depth. In large part, the reason that this devotion did not find a home in the East is that the theological approach to Christ is different in the East than in the West. For the West, the sacrifice of Jesus on the cross is the primary focus (this is why the

Mass is called "*the Sacrifice* of the Mass"). There are two aspects to every Mass and every Divine Liturgy; they could be called the "primary themes" of these services of worship. They are the death and resurrection of Jesus.

The West has looked at the death of Jesus as primary, while the East has looked at the resurrection as primary. This is why, for example, the processional cross in Byzantine Churches has two sides: one is the crucified Lord while the other side shows the resurrected Lord. On Sundays, little Paschas, or Easters, the side of the resurrection is always shown.

78. Do Eastern Catholics pray the rosary?

The short answer is that some do and some don't. Because of the incursion of latinizations (not just in the United States, but also in the Middle East), many Eastern Catholics have adopted this private devotion and made it their own. There is nothing wrong with this, of course, and there has been no attempt to remove the rosary from the devotional practices of Eastern Catholics.

At the same time, this is a *private* devotion and, therefore, the Eastern Catholic Churches do not (or should not) have public recitation of the rosary in church. This has happened (especially in the Ukrainian Churches), but the practice is discouraged.

79. I went to a Lenten retreat at an Eastern Catholic Church, and the priest and deacon were "praying like Muslims." Why did they do that?

By "praying like Muslims," I'm assuming you mean the prayer posture. You could also mean praying in Arabic, and this would be the case if the church were from a Middle Eastern area where Arabic was the common language. In fact, since *Allah* is simply the Arabic word for "God," it is quite likely that you did hear them praying to Allah.

If, however, you are referring to posture, then we need to do a little explaining. The posture commonly associated with

Muslim prayer is the head touching the ground and the hindquarters in the air. That is, kneeling and then touching the head to the ground without lying down. This is an ancient prayer position called a "great metany" and is found in ancient Christian practice in the Middle East and elsewhere.

The great metany is, like the little metany (see Question 70), a sign of repentance, of conversion, of acknowledgment of sins and failures. The most common time that one sees this is during Great Lent in the Prayer of Saint Ephrem.[25] Both great metanies and little metanies are made during this prayer.

80. I heard that Eastern Catholic priests can get married. Is that true?

Once a man has been ordained to the diaconate, he may not marry. However, a married man may be ordained to the priesthood. That part is true. Let's add a little history to this. Going back to the very beginning of the church, we know that Saint Peter was married since his mother-in-law is mentioned in Scripture. In the letter to Timothy, ascribed to Saint Paul, it specifies that a man who is being considered for ecclesial office (bishop, priest, deacon) should not have been married more than once. Eventually, the office of bishop was reserved to monastics, which, by definition, meant men who were not married.

The Latin Church enacted several different laws that, from the latter fourth century, created a celibate priesthood. This remains the current discipline in the Latin Church, although there may be exceptions made for Anglican/Episcopalian and Lutheran ministers who become Catholic and who wish to continue their ministry. These are evaluated on a case-by-case basis, and there are currently married Latin Rite priests who became priests under this exception. The basic teaching of the church is that marriage is not an impediment (block) to orders but, rather, that orders is an impediment to marriage.

In the United States and Canada, however, there was a protocol (an agreement) that said that because the vast majority of Catholics in those two countries were Latin Rite, the Eastern Catholic Churches would not ordain married men, nor would they bring married priests from the "old country" to serve here. This protocol was enacted following the tragic circumstances following the arrival of Father Alexis Toth, a widowed priest, in 1889.

During the mid-1880s, the Slavic Byzantine Church had established several parishes in the United States and needed priests to staff them. Because there were no Eastern bishops here, these parishes fell under the good graces of the Latin bishops of the diocese in which they were located. The first problem arose in Philadelphia, where Father John Volyansky, a married priest, was denied the faculties to celebrate the sacraments (the speculation is that this was because he was married). Around the same time, Father Toth was assigned to serve the people in Minneapolis. He was a canon (while there are canons in the Latin Church, the term generally refers to a monastic, while in the East this is a position of authority just below that of a bishop) and expected to be treated with a certain amount of dignity. Neither he nor Archbishop John Ireland, the bishop of Minneapolis at the time, seemed to understand the position of the other. The result was that Father Toth was told his services were not needed, and that a local Polish priest would serve the Slavic community.

Archbishop Ireland had already sent a request to Rome in an effort to prevent married (or, it seems, even widowed) priests from coming to the United States. Eventually, as a result of the problems Father Toth encountered, he left the Catholic Church and, with the people he was sent to serve, became Orthodox. He is considered a saint of the Orthodox Church.

However, Rome was very concerned with the situation and did, in fact, enact "particular law" that prevented married priests from serving in the United States or Canada. That particular law is generally considered to have been abolished with the Decree on the Catholic Churches of the Eastern Rite. This was, in fact, tested by the

Melkite Church when a married man was ordained to the priesthood for the United States. Several married men have since been ordained to the priesthood, and numerous married priests have come from the Middle East to serve parishes in the United States and Canada.

81. My neighbor is a Melkite deacon, and I noticed they called his wife a "deaconessa." Do Eastern Catholic Churches have female deacons?

No, there are no female deacons in the Eastern Catholic Churches (although, interestingly enough, there were in the long distant past, and the Church of England currently ordains women not only to the diaconate, but also as priests and bishops). The wife of a clergyman in the Eastern Churches acquires a title because of her marriage. The term *deaconessa* simply means that she is married to a deacon.

82. What is a presbytera?

As we noted in the previous question, the wife of a clergyman acquires a title by virtue of her marriage. A *presbytera* (or, sometimes, *presbutera*) is the wife of a priest—this is the Greek title since it comes from the Greek word *presbyteros,* which is the Scriptural term for an elder. It is the root from which *presbyter* is derived, the order to which a man is ordained and whom we call a priest. If she were in a Slavic Church, she would be called "Matushka," while in an Arabic Church she would be "Khouria." As we noted in Question 81, the deacon's wife is "Deaconessa," and this seems to hold across linguistic differentiation.

83. If the Catholic Church is "one, holy, catholic, and apostolic," why is it that the East does things so differently from the West? Why can't we all be the same?

Why doesn't everyone like a particular food, or a particular type of music? The Catholic Church is *one* because we share the same faith, not because we do everything the same way. Uniformity of faith is a requirement for membership in the church, but uniformity of practice is not now — and *never* has been — a part of our church traditions.

Let's go back in time to the days of the apostles to see if we can't put a handle on this. When the apostles went out from Jerusalem to preach the good news, the people they went to had different traditions and different languages (even though most were subjects of the Roman emperors). The liturgical starting point for Eastern worship seems to have been the Divine Liturgy of Saint James, from which all other liturgies are derived (or, at least, that's the thinking of many, but not all, scholars).

Ancient tradition tells us that Saint Mark went to Alexandria, from which we later get the Divine Liturgy of Saint Mark. That Liturgy was, in turn, modified for the Ethiopians and later for the Ge'ez (pronounced "Gaze") Church in Eritrea. Why was it modified? Well, language would be one reason. All early Liturgies were celebrated (in the East we normally say "served") in the language of the people.

Both Saint Paul and Saint Peter went to Antioch, and the people probably followed a Greek Liturgy. Later the Melkites would follow the Byzantine custom — again, because of the influence of the government and the trade routes. Later, under the influence of the Muslims, they shifted to Arabic.

From popular tradition we believe that Saint Thomas went to India, where the Christians call themselves "St. Thomas Christians." They developed their own linguistic variations on the Liturgy. Unfortunately, due to the vagaries of history, we know very little about the early Liturgy used there. Today St. Thomas Christians are part of the Syriac tradition.

The Liturgy in Rome was originally in Greek, and only in the fourth century did it shift to Latin, and that was a slow process. Because "all roads lead to Rome" the Liturgy here was influenced especially by Milan in the fourth and fifth centuries. And, conversely, when German pilgrims came to Rome, they returned to their homes using the Gallic Rite. Charlemagne imposed the Roman Rite on his subjects in central Europe. This was of great influence in the West, while the East continued to develop their own traditions.

The development of the Liturgy, and other religious practices, was a slow but continuous process for at least the first six hundred years of the church. After that, the East was dealing with the Muslim occupation; changes in the Liturgy were very few after that event, although hymns used in monastic circles were placed in the Liturgy, causing it to become very long.

The Second Vatican Council has affirmed the validity and importance of the Eastern Catholic Churches.[26] Pope John Paul II referred to the Eastern Churches as the "other lung" of the church.[27] For all these reasons, and many more, it's important that we *not* all do the same thing the same way. Rather, the faith is revealed in all its wonderful depth and mystery through the many and varied ways in which it is expressed.

84. What are Eastern Catholic wedding ceremonies like?

We speak of Eastern "marriage ceremonies," because there are at least two ceremonies and, in some cases, three! The first is the betrothal or engagement ceremony, the second is the crowning ceremony (see Question 52), and the third is the "removal of the crowns" that takes place after the honeymoon.

In the betrothal ceremony, the blessing of the bride and the groom and the exchange of rings takes place. If we remember the story of Joseph and Mary in Scripture, we recall that they were betrothed and that this was far more than just the engagement of the civil society around us. This is because this ceremony is actually blessed by the church and in the church. The way in which this is carried out varies from one ritual church to another, but the elements of the exchange of rings (done by the priest) and the blessing of the couple are the significant elements.

The actual marriage ceremony takes place outside of the Divine Liturgy in the Byzantine tradition but within the Liturgy for the Copts and Maronites. In the Byzantine Church there is no giving of consent as part of the rite. This is done before the marriage ceremony in those countries (such as the United States) that have giving of consent as a part of the legal requirements for marriage. Even when this exchange of vows takes place at the same time as the marriage ceremony, it's always before the priest says, "Blessed is the kingdom of the Father, and the Son, and the Holy Spirit, now and always and forever and ever" (or, in some translations, "now and ever and unto ages of ages"), which is the formal beginning of the Liturgy.

85. Are Eastern Catholic ordination ceremonies the same as Roman Catholic ordinations?

In the sense that they all involve a laying on of hands, the answer is yes, they are the same. However, there are significant differences as well. One example of a difference is that in the East there are generally neither prostrations nor a chanting of the litany of saints. Even among the various Eastern Churches there are differences in the ordination ceremonies. For example, in the Byzantine tradition a man being ordained a deacon is led up to the bishop and is walked around the altar or holy table three times to represent his role of service. This does not happen in the Maronite tradition.

When a man is ordained a priest in the Byzantine tradition, he is led around the church by two deacons (the order he is leaving) and brought to the holy doors (doing three *metanies* or bows along the way), where the bishop greets him. After he is ordained he is led into the altar area by two priests who walk him around the holy table.

The Eastern Churches have retained the role of the subdeacon, and his ordination is somewhat different because it happens in the nave and not in the "sanctuary" or area behind the iconostasis.

86. What are the vestments a bishop wears? A priest? A deacon? What vestments do other clergy and ministers wear?

This is a difficult question to answer because it varies from church to church. Generally, we can say that all churches, Eastern and Western, wear a long robe. In the West it's called an "alb," and most of the East uses the older Greek term *sticharion*. This is the vestment proper to all grades of orders, and is even worn by the altar servers. In the Latin and Syriac Churches, it tends to be white, while in the Byzantine Churches it is the color of the vestments to be worn (red, green, and so on). For a priest or bishop this is very plain, but for a deacon or subdeacon (at least, in the Byzantine tradition) it is very ornate since it is not covered by anything. Deacons wear cuffs (called *epimanikia* in Greek or *zende* in the Syriac tradition) that go inside the sticharion.

Bishops, priests, deacons, and subdeacons wear a stole, although, as in the Latin Church, this varies by grade. Subdeacons in the Syriac Churches (including the Maronites) wear a long strip of cloth that hangs down the back and front on the left side and loops under the right arm, crossing chest and back. This is also the diaconal stole (called an *orarion*) worn by all Melkite deacons and by protodeacons in the Ruthenian and other Slavic Byzantine Churches. Syriac deacons and deacons of the Slavic Byzantine Churches wear a long strip of cloth that simply hangs from the left shoulder down the front and the back.

Moving on to priests, their stole (called an *epitrachelion* in the Greek tradition and *hamnikho* in the Syriac) looks much like a Latin Rite priest's stole except that it is sewn together to form a solid band, leaving an opening for it to be slipped over the priest's head. This is common to all Eastern Churches. Syriac priests wear what in the West would be called a "cope," while Byzantine priests wear a *phelonian,* which looks much like a chasuble except that it is shorter in front than in back. There is also a belt (called a *zone* in the Byzantine tradition or *zenoro* in the Syriac tradition) that is worn, and the epitrachelion goes under the belt.

Some priests are given the honor of wearing what looks like a diamond-shaped shield called an *epigonation*. Priests also wear cuffs, but these go over the sticharion.

Bishops in the Syriac tradition are vested much as priests except that they also wear a pallium and a *masnaphato* or turban. Maronite bishops vary slightly from this in that they generally do not wear the masnaphato, replacing it with the miter, and do not wear the pallium. Byzantine bishops wear everything a priest wears except the phelonian, replacing that with a *sakkos* (which looks much like a Latin Rite dalmatic). They also wear an *omophorion,* which is a very large stole. It wraps around the bishop's neck, is draped across the chest, and hangs down the left side in front and in back.

All bishops wear some sort of pectoral cross, but this cross is not specific to the bishop since priests may be given the honor to wear one and, in fact, all Russian priests wear them. So the bishop also wears one or two medallions (called *encolpia*).

As with the Latin Rite, clergy in the East have special "choir dress" that is usually a cassock and, if permitted, a cross. Melkite clergy traditionally will, if present at Liturgy and not serving, wear just a cassock (called a *rason* or *jibby*) and put on their stole to go to communion.

87. At a recent event, the priest (from an Eastern Catholic Church) wore some kind of round hat with a veil, and the deacon wore a round hat without a veil. What's the significance of this? I thought only bishops wore "hats" in church!

This is a good question! No, clearly bishops are *not* the only ones who wear "hats" in church. The bishop is the one most commonly seen wearing a miter (hat) or a *zucchetto* (the yarmulke-like skullcap). However, before the Second Vatican Council one might see a priest enter the church wearing a *biretta*. This is a hat with three stiff ridges or spines on the top and a pompom in the center. This particular item has fallen somewhat into disuse in the Latin Church, although it is still permitted.

Eastern clergy are also permitted to wear specific head coverings. The "hat" you describe is of Greek usage, so it would be most commonly found in the Byzantine tradition. Because it's Greek, it has a Greek name: *kamelavkion*. This is a cylindrical hat that may have either a peaked top or a flat top, and there may or may not be a rim at the top. The presence of a veil indicates that the wearer is a monk, a bishop, or a priest with an honor that permits him to wear the veil.

Russian clerics have a slightly different hat, called a *kamalavai*, which is also cylindrical, but tapered with the narrow portion at the head. It is always flat on top. This hat is normally black, but Russian bishops may wear white as well (since the Russian Catholic Church has no hierarchy at this time, the only way one sees this is by looking at the Russian Orthodox Church). There is also a "soft hat" called a *skoufia*, which looks more like a military barracks cap. This comes in different colors: purple indicates the wearer has received a special honor or title; black is the usual color.

In the Syriac Church the "hat" is really a hood that is covered with stars and worn tightly over the head by monks, or a *phiro* (sort of like a black zucchetto) for other priests. Other ritual churches have vestments that are particular to their origins.

And, finally, bishops do wear "hats" too! However, in the East this is usually a crown or corona. Yet, there are some Eastern bishops (such as the Maronites) who wear a miter that is identical to those worn by Latin Rite bishops.

I should also mention that priests in the Eastern Catholics Churches may be given the honor to wear a pectoral cross. This does not mean that they are bishops (see Question 86). All Russian Catholic priests may wear crosses. Other Byzantine priests may wear a cross if they have been given that honor (either to wear the cross or, by virtue of title, to wear a cross).

As an aside, in the Coptic and Indian Churches it is traditional for the people to remove their shoes before entering the church. The clergy wear special slippers called *msone*.

88. I noticed that Eastern Catholic Churches use a significantly different architecture from that of Latin Churches. Why is that?

In part the differences in architecture are due to various climatic and cultural differences. For example, the "onion domes" of Russian Churches are based upon the Byzantine dome of other Byzantine Churches, but shaped so as to shed snow (it snows in Russia a lot more than it does in, say, Greece). This shape is also seen as the flame of a candle reaching to heaven. Other differences reflect a different theological perspective in the role of the church building.

The primary difference is the use of a dome as opposed to the vaulted ceilings of the Gothic Churches of Europe, the use of an iconostasis as opposed to an altar rail or, as in so many churches today, nothing between the nave and sanctuary. If we look at these we can see that they are simply different expressions of how we relate to God.

The vaulted ceiling is designed to draw one's eyes upward, to view the vast separation between man and God. It represents, in short, the "transcendence" of God. God's power, majesty, and awe are reflected in this design. In fact, when the king of England first viewed Westminster Cathedral, he told the architect that it was "awful, pompous and artificial" — meaning, of course, that it was "full of awe, stately and majestic, and man-made."

The Byzantine tradition, however, stresses the "immanence" of God. The dome represents his arms outstretched over us, protecting us, being with us. Normally the inside of the dome is covered with iconography, so that we are seeing a view into heaven where God hears the saints interceding for us. In fact, most Orthodox and Byzantine Catholic Churches have an icon of the

Pantokrator, which reveals Jesus as the "Creator of All." At the end of the Divine Liturgy we pray, "Through the prayers of our holy fathers, O Lord Jesus Christ, have mercy on us and save us."

The iconostasis (East) and the altar rail (West) actually serve the same purpose. They are to set off the holy place from the nave of the church. This "holy place" represents heaven, while the nave represents and is, in fact, earth. There are usually statues in the sanctuary of Latin Churches, and these may be seen as corresponding to the icons on the iconostasis (they don't actually have the same theological significance, but for our purposes can be seen in the same light).

89. My Eastern Catholic coworker always has a rope with knots tied in it around her wrist. Is that an Eastern rosary?

Well, yes, in a way. What you saw is called a "prayer rope" or, in Slavic tradition, a *chotki.* Unlike the rosary of the West, which traditionally has five sets of ten beads, plus an additional bead between three of these groups, and still more beads (one, three, and one) by the crucifix, the prayer rope may have a varying number of beads all next to each other. Traditionally this will be 33, 50, 100, 150, or even 300 knots that form the beads. The cross is also formed from knots, and there is a real art to tying these prayer ropes.

Also, unlike the rosary, the prayer that is said on these prayer ropes is the "Jesus Prayer" ("Lord Jesus Christ, Son of God, have mercy on me a sinner"). Note, however, that the Ukrainian Church has a particular devotion to the rosary just as does the Latin Church, and many Eastern Catholics, because they grow up in schools taught by Latin Rite priests or nuns, may also have a devotion to praying the rosary.

Many Middle Eastern people carry what looks like a type of rosary with square "beads" that have writing on them and that form a circle with no cross. This is neither a prayer rope nor a rosary—it's the Muslim "worry beads." Even though Christians may say prayers on them, they are just using them to keep their hands occupied. Many contend, however, that this is also of Christian origin, since there are always thirty-three or ninety-nine beads, with the thirty-three being the number of years that Jesus is said to have lived on Earth and the ninety-nine representing the threefold manifestation of those years (Father, Son, and Holy Spirit, so 3 times 33 yields 99).

90. Is there any difference between the way Roman Catholics go to confession and the way Eastern Catholics go to confession?

Yes and no. First, both do an examination of conscience before receiving the sacrament of reconciliation, as it is called in the West—but then the differences come into play. In the Byzantine tradition, most people simply ask the priest to hear their confession (usually before a Liturgy), and they go and stand in front of the icon of Christ. There the penitent confesses his or her sins to Christ while the priest "listens in." The priest may then offer some counseling and a penance. Then the penitent kneels while the priest, laying his epitrachelion on the head of the penitent, says the prayer of absolution.

There are generally no confessionals or "chambers of reconciliation" in Eastern churches, so this takes the place of one. Because people are aware of this custom, they generally keep back when they see a person going to confession.

91. My child was baptized by a deacon in the Roman Catholic Church. Is that possible in the Eastern Catholic Churches?

The short answer is, It all depends! If the deacon is a Maronite deacon, then yes, it can happen. However, if he is Byzantine, the answer is no, unless the child is in danger of death. Because the mysteries of initiation (baptism, Eucharist, and chrismation) are all intimately linked, most Eastern Churches celebrate these together. Thus, only a priest or bishop normally baptizes. And baptism is immediately followed by giving the child first communion and then chrismation (confirmation in the West).

92. Are the roles of the priest and deacon the same in the Eastern Catholic Church as they are in the Roman Catholic Church?

The answer to this question depends on the meaning of the term *role*. If it refers to the functions of the priest and deacon, then, no, they are not. The role of the priest is virtually identical in both sets of churches, although in the East he also takes on more of the role of spiritual father. This role was common in the West up until the late 1950s or early 1960s, when the increase in the number of Latin Rite Catholics made this function more difficult for the priest, at least in terms of knowing all his parishioners as a spiritual father.

The role of the deacon in the Eastern Churches, especially of the Byzantine tradition, is much more active in the Liturgy than is the Latin deacon. Eastern deacons are continually going in and out of the holy place to lead the people in prayer (usually chanted litanies). In the Byzantine tradition, the deacon is the one who elevates the *diskos* (paten) and *poterion* (chalice) after the consecration. The deacon does most of the incensing, too. The deacon also directs the priest as the Liturgy progresses, starting with "It is time for the Lord to act" before Liturgy starts, to his command "Give the blessing father/master" (the latter is for a bishop) at the start of Liturgy. During the Liturgy itself, he tells the priest to "bless the holy bread…bless the chalice" and other directives. His role of charity and service is, or should be, the same as that of a Latin Rite deacon.

Deacons may not witness marriages—the theology of the East is that the priest or bishop is the minister of the Mystery of Holy Crowning (matrimony) and, thus, the deacon may not witness the marriage. Deacons also do not bless (other than in the same way that a layperson blesses). Thus, one may not bring an object or person to a deacon to be blessed. Deacons do not, therefore, do house blessings.

The proper way to bless an icon is not for a priest or bishop to bless it, but to set it on the altar during the Liturgy. There is a long tradition in the East that things are blessed by usage. Thus, using something in a holy fashion will bless that thing. Icons, because they represent a window into heaven, are most appropriately a part of the Divine Liturgy that makes heaven and earth touch, and, therefore, are blessed through the action of the Liturgy itself.

93. What about the role of the bishop?

The role of the bishop is slightly different because, unlike the Latin bishop, he doesn't have to go from parish to parish administering confirmation. However, most Eastern bishops still try to visit every parish in their eparchy (diocese) each year. This can be made more difficult in light of the size of some of the eparchies. For example, the Romanian Eparchy of Canton and the Melkite Eparchy of Newton both encompass the entire United States!

The Eastern bishop is seen as a father and head of the community in a way that is perhaps more tangible than in the West. The deacon commemorates him in the Byzantine Liturgy by asking the people to pray for "our father and (Arch) Bishop N," which calls to mind his role as the head of the local church. This should be the same as the Latin Church, where he is commemorated in the eucharistic prayer ("for our bishop N"), but it seems more common for communities in the East to have a closer relationship with their bishops.

This relationship comes from the fact that, in general, Eastern bishops are more accessible to their people. They publish their phone numbers and frequently answer their own phones! They also make a point of meeting with as many of their people as they can when they visit, usually spending several days at a given parish. Latin bishops generally do not have the luxury of doing this because they are administering their diocese and, as a result, are not able to develop close relationships with the lay-people in their communities.

94. My Eastern Catholic friend had to leave a meeting the other day for a house blessing. Can you explain that?

House blessings are a custom in many parts of the world. Filipinos are among the most frequent requestors for house bless-ings in the Latin Church, but there are others who also seek out this special favor from God on their dwellings. In the Eastern Church, most priests attempt to visit every family in their parish at least once a year and, at the same time, will bless the house. This provides an opportunity for the community's local "spiritual father" to visit, break bread, and provide personal assurance of the love and care that the church has for her people.

95. As part of my RCIA formation, we went to an Eastern Catholic Church. I noticed that the altar servers were getting their robes blessed before they put them on. Is that usual, or were these just new robes?

Not only the servers, but *all* ministers have their vestments blessed before the Liturgy! The bishop or priest, of course, blesses his own vestment. The deacon, subdeacon, and servers will ask the bishop or, in his absence, the priest to bless their vestments before Liturgy. Servers and subdeacons simply fold the vestments and present them for blessing. The deacon specifically asks, "Bless, master, the sticharion and orarion" (there is no mention of the cuffs or epimanikia). It's not that the blessing will "wear off," but that this act reminds us that what we are about to do is the Lord's work and, as such, it is holy and we, too, should be holy.

At this point we should also note that there are vesting prayers associated with the vestment. This was clearly the case in the Latin Church before the Second Vatican Council, but these prayers seem to have fallen into disuse—partly because certain of the vestments of the Latin Church have disappeared: the maniple (which started out as a napkin and remained as a symbol of service over the left arm of the subdeacon, deacon, priest, or bishop) and the amice (a small rectangle of white linen that was worn over the shoulders by the subdeacon, deacon, priest, and bishop). Latin vestments were to be blessed prior to their first use, so the blessing of vestments is not unique to the East. The vesting prayers may still be said by the deacon, priest, or bishop for those items that are still in use, and are always said in the East (although there is no vesting prayer for the orarion or deacon's stole in the Byzantine tradition—the deacon simply kisses the orarion where one of the crosses is sewn on it).

96. Where is the tabernacle in an Eastern Catholic Church?

The tabernacle, called an *artiphorion,* is usually on the altar or, if it is shaped like a dove, suspended above the altar. Unlike the Latin tabernacle, however, it is usually very small, as it is used to preserve only a single piece of Eucharist (the Lamb) from Holy Thursday (at least, this is the Byzantine tradition). In the Maronite Church, you will usually find it behind the altar, although it is often built into something else so is not as visible.

Eastern Churches, because there is no tradition of eucharistic devotion (see Question 74) do not reserve the Eucharist for that purpose, and this allows the artiphorion to be small. But, since the Eucharist is reserved for taking communion to the sick, there may actually be a second artiphorion for that purpose and it, too, will be on the altar. This second artiphorion is required because the main artiphorion contains only the piece of the Lamb from Holy Thursday.

97. Why don't Eastern Catholics kneel during the consecration?

Generally, Eastern parishes follow the directives of the Council of Nicaea that prohibit kneeling on Sundays. In Eastern theology kneeling is a sign of penance, not of adoration. In the East the normal posture of prayer is standing, and it is this that directs us. Kneeling *does* take place in Eastern Churches, but this is in keeping with the spirit of Great Lent when one becomes a penitent, or as is done when going to confession (see Question 90).

98. Is genuflecting a part of the Eastern Catholic tradition?

No, it is not. The word *genuflect* comes from two Latin words: *genu,* which means "knee," and *flectere,* which means "to bend." This action arises out of Latin practice and never made inroads into Eastern tradition. That's not to say that there is no Eastern practice that corresponds to this.

The most common, and one that has been mentioned in Questions 70 and 79, is the *metany* or bow. There are different grades or degrees of metanies, but they are used where, in the West, people would genuflect. There are other places where the custom is different. For example, it used to be a custom in the Latin Church to genuflect on the left knee before the bishop or pope and then to kiss his ring. In the Eastern Church one cups one's hands together and bows before the bishop (or priest) and asks, "Bless, Master" (or, for a priest, "Bless, Father"). Then one kisses the right hand of the bishop (or priest). When priests greet each other, they traditionally kiss each other's hand.

In fact, this hand kissing takes place a number of times during the Liturgy, when the deacon, on receiving a blessing, kisses the hand of the priest or bishop who gave the blessing or after he receives communion. People will often kiss the hand of the deacon, who, like the priest, dispenses the Word of God and the Eucharist.

But this is drifting afar from the original question. Genuflecting is not a part of the Eastern practice at all (but may be done by those who, growing up in the Latin tradition, find it appropriate).

99. Do Eastern clergy have to pray the Liturgy of the Hours?

As soon as the words *have to* appeared in this question, I got the shakes. The reason for that is the Eastern Churches tend to avoid the whole concept of "obligation" entirely. For the East it is no more mandatory to pray than it is to, say, breathe or eat. All three are necessary for life and so should be done with great regularity.

Now, having said that, the answer is that all clergy are supposed to "pray constantly." The East does, indeed, have a type of Liturgy of the Hours, but it is not the same as the Latin Church's prayer. In fact, it is far more complicated, as the form that has come down to us today originated in the monasteries and is better suited to the rhythm of life that is found there.

The normal worship book used by the Byzantine Rite, at least in the United States, is called *Byzantine Daily Worship*. It contains the prayers for Vespers, Compline, Matins, Lauds, Prime, Terce, Sext, and None. These hours are almost always said by the monastics.

EPILOGUE

Jesus reigned from the beginning over the few who believed in
Him, and in the end He will reign over all the world.
—Saint Aphrahat, the Persian sage,
The Demonstrations of Aphrahat

100. What do Eastern Catholics think about being in communion with Rome?

Based upon my dialogue with both clergy and laity in many of the Eastern Catholic Churches, I have to say that for most Eastern Catholics, it's not an issue. There is little or no consideration given to the Church of Rome or the pope since they don't affect their everyday lives. In that regard, the pope is probably treated about the same as many Roman Catholics would treat him or think about him. They pray for him, especially in the Divine Liturgy, and look to him as a spiritual father.

For clergy, however, this question is more meaningful. For many there is a sense of unease, of not knowing what Rome will do to or for the Eastern Churches. While the pope has always been supportive of Eastern Catholics, the same cannot be said for the various congregations that, over the years, have been supportive, indifferent, or downright hostile. There is also resentment over the way in which Rome deals with some of the issues that are seen as belonging to a particular ritual church. These are matters that are now dealt with through the Congregation of Eastern Churches.

But the bottom line is this: Communion with Rome was a hallmark of the church for the first thousand years, and it is seen by all Eastern Catholic Churches as important. Thus, no matter how difficult things may get at times with Rome, this is part of who we all are as Catholics. This union, although flawed by not including all the Orthodox, is a positive step. We await the time when, heeding the words of Jesus' prayer for unity, we can resolve our differences and be once again what we were for the first thousand years of our history. We can put aside any rancor, any distrust, any sense of "us" and "them," and be a true sign to the world of what it means to be "one, holy, catholic, and apostolic."

At the same time, we have to acknowledge that union with Rome has been beneficial. Among the very first benefits to such a union was the enhancements made possible in the education of the clergy. Interestingly enough, Rome has also provided a layer of protection for the customs and traditions of the Eastern Catholic Churches so that these were not lost, especially in North America, where there was a tendency to incorporate practices, actions, and prayers from the West to either replace or supplement authentic Eastern traditions.

101. When do you expect the Roman Catholic Church and Orthodox Church to reunite?

The short answer is that I expect this to happen before the *parousia* or second coming of Christ! The long answer is that it took us two thousand years to get to where we arc today. Of that, nearly one thousand years have gone by since the year in which nothing happened (1054). During that time, the Church of Rome has reached out to the East on numerous occasions, but always on Western terms. The dialogue that is happening today is good and beneficial. Lay societies such as the Society of St. John Chrysostom are doing much good work in helping both sides to understand what the problems and difficulties are, and are actively working toward better understanding.

This is a long-standing problem, and there are many issues to be resolved and details to be worked out. It will take a very long time for any reunion to happen. I know that Pope John Paul II, of blessed memory, had wanted this before his death, but it may take a hundred years or more to get to that point. This is, of course, just as guess.

Any reunion that takes place in a short period of time will not have addressed the pertinent issues sufficiently and, like the reunion brokered at Florence, will eventually—and unfortunately—fail. Fortunately, there is ongoing dialogue on both local and international levels. In fact, it was recently announced by both Rome and Constantinople that the international dialogue will be resuming shortly. This dialogue has led to a common vocabulary that allows participants from both sides to discuss theological or practical issues knowing that the terms mean the same things.

Beginning with the mutual lifting of the excommunications by Pope Paul VI and Patriarch Athenagoras in 1965, there has been an ongoing series of events—both meetings and shared prayer—between the Latin Church and the Orthodox Church that can only lead to greater understanding and, eventually, to reunion. Both sides are committed to and understand that this is a long-term process and will work forward with that understanding. In fact, as this book is being written, there is evidence that the relations between the Russian Orthodox Church and the Catholic Church are beginning to thaw.

Finally, the best answer is, I think, found in the last two words in Alexandre Dumas's *The Count of Monte Cristo:* Wait and hope!

NOTES

1. The union with the Chaldeans was due to an interesting fluke of history. In 1551, Catholicos Shim'un V died, leaving only an eight-year-old boy, his nephew. Since the position of catholicos was hereditary, it should have been passed on to this boy, who was eventually installed as Shim'un VI by the hierarchy. However, three metropolitans did not like the idea of such a young boy as catholicos. Therefore, they gathered together with like-minded clergy and selected Yuhanna Sulaqa as catholicos. Since there were now two people holding that title, it was decided to go to Rome to get a definitive resolution. Sulaqa and one noble went to Rome, where Sulaqa was quizzed about his faith to ensure he was orthodox. He misled the pope with regard to the presence of a catholicos and, after making a profession of faith, was given the pallium by Pope Julius III. This whole story can be read in greater detail in *Catholics and Sultans* by Charles Frazee (New York: Cambridge University Press, 1983, 55–58).

2. This whole question of uniatism is far more complex than we can get into in this short book. For more on this, see Archimandrite Robert Taft, SJ, *Anamnesis, Not Amnesia: The "Healing Memories" and the Problem of "Uniatism,"* 21st Kelly Lecture, University of St. Michael's College, Toronto, Canada (December 1, 2000). A more detailed examination of this is found in Ernst C. Suttner's *Church Unity: Union or Uniatism? Catholic-Orthodox Ecumenical Perspectives* (Rome: Centre for Indian and Interreligious Studies and Bangalore: Dhamaram Publications, 1991).

3. Acts 2:43–47: "Awe came upon everyone, because many wonders and signs were being done by the apostles. All who believed were together and had all things in common; they would sell their possessions and goods and distribute the proceeds to all, as any had need. Day by day, as they spent much time together in the temple, they broke bread at home and ate their food with glad and generous hearts, praising God and having the goodwill of all the people. And day by day the Lord added to their number those who were being saved."

4. Acts 17:22–25: "Then Paul stood in front of the Areopagus and said, 'Athenians, I see how extremely religious you are in every way. For as I went through the city and looked carefully at the objects of your worship, I found among them an altar with the inscription, "To an unknown god." What therefore you worship as unknown, this I proclaim to you. The God who made the world and everything in it, he who is Lord of heaven and earth, does not live in shrines made by human hands, nor is he served by human hands, as though he needed anything, since he himself gives to all mortals life and breath and all things.'"

5. "As therefore the Lord does nothing without the Father, for says He, 'I can of mine own self do nothing,' so do ye, neither presbyter, nor deacon, nor layman, do anything without the bishop. Nor let anything appear commendable to you which is destitute of his approval. For every such thing is sinful, and opposed [to the will of] God. Do ye all come together into the same place for prayer. Let there be one common supplication, one mind, one hope, with faith unblameable in Christ Jesus, than which nothing is more excellent. Do ye all, as one man, run together into the temple of God, as unto one altar, to one Jesus Christ, the High Priest of the unbegotten God" (Saint Ignatius of Antioch, *Epistle to the Magnesians*).

6. See *Apostolicae Curae* (On the Nullity of Anglican Orders), September 18, 1896.

7. For more on this period, there are several good histories of the early church. One such is Henry Chandwick's *The Early Church* (New York: Penguin Books, 1967), which covers the period from the founding of the church through the events of 1054. For greater detail on the development of the theology of

this period, there is no finer reference work that that of Professor Jaroslav Pelikan, *The Christian Tradition: A History of the Development of Doctrine, Volume 1: The Emergence of the Catholic Tradition (100–600)* (Chicago: University of Chicago Press, 1975). This is part of a five-volume work on the early church. Volume 3 of this collection picks up in the year 600 and carries through to the year 1300. Volume 2 deals with the development of Eastern spirituality from 600 to 1700.

8. Canon 43: "The bishop of the Church of Rome, in whom resides the office *(munus)* given in special way by the Lord to Peter, first of the Apostles and to be transmitted to his successors, is head of the college of bishops, the Vicar of Christ and Pastor of the entire Church on earth; therefore, in virtue of his office *(munus)* he enjoys supreme, full, immediate and universal ordinary power in the Church which he can always freely exercise" (Code of Canons of the Eastern Churches).

Canon 331: "The office uniquely committed by the Lord to Peter, the first of the Apostles, and to be transmitted to his successors, abides in the Bishop of the Church of Rome. He is the head of the College of Bishops, the Vicar of Christ, and the Pastor of the universal Church here on earth. Consequently, by virtue of his office, he has supreme, full, immediate and universal ordinary power in the Church, and he can always freely exercise this power" (Code of Canons of the Eastern Churches).

9. Canon 63: "A patriarch is canonically elected in the synod of bishops of the patriarchal Church" (Code of Canons of the Eastern Churches).

10. Canon 72 §2: "If the election is not brought to completion within fifteen days from the opening of the synod of bishops, the matter devolves to the Roman Pontiff" (Code of Canons of the Eastern Churches).

11. Canon 153 §1: "A major archbishop is elected according to the norm of canons 63–74."

§2: "After the election has been accepted by the person elected, the synod of bishops of the major archepiscopal Church must inform the Roman Pontiff with a synodal letter about the canonical election; the person who has been elected must, in a letter signed in his own hand, petition the confirmation of his election by the Roman Pontiff" (Code of Canons of the Eastern Churches).

12. See 2 Peter 1:4.

13. Exodus 20:4–5: "You shall not make for yourself an idol, whether in the form of anything that is in heaven above, or that is on the earth beneath, or that is in the water under the earth. You shall not bow down to them or worship them; for I the LORD your God am a jealous God, punishing children for the iniquity of parents, to the third and the fourth generation of those who reject me."

14. "By her relationship with Christ, the Church is a kind of sacrament or sign of intimate union with God, and of the unity of all mankind" (*Lumen Gentium* (Dogmatic Constitution on the Church), §1).

15. 775: "'The Church, in Christ, is like a sacrament—a sign and instrument, that is, of communion with God and of unity among all men.' The Church's first purpose is to be the sacrament of the inner union of men with God. Because men's communion with one another is rooted in that union with God, the Church is also the sacrament of the unity of the human race. In her, this unity is already begun, since she gathers men 'from every nation, from all tribes and peoples and tongues'; at the same time, the Church is the 'sign and instrument' of the full realization of the unity yet to come" *(Catechism of the Catholic Church).*

776: "As sacrament, the Church is Christ's instrument. 'She is taken up by him also as the instrument for the salvation of all,' 'the universal sacrament of salvation,' by which Christ is 'at once manifesting and actualizing the mystery of God's love for men.' The Church 'is the visible plan of God's love for humanity,' because God desires 'that the whole human race may become one People of God, form one Body of Christ, and be built up into one temple of the Holy Spirit'" *(Catechism of the Catholic Church).*

16. Saint Augustine, *The Enchiridion or On Faith, Hope and Love Addressed to Laurentius,* chap. 28.

17. See Genesis 1:26.

18. *Summa Theologica,* Question 27, Article 1, Reply to Objection 1.

19. The Divine Liturgy of Saint John Chrysostom.

20. Ibid.

21. Ibid.

22. "Thou therefore, O bishop, according to that type, shalt anoint the head of those that are to be baptized, whether they be men or women, with the holy oil, for a type of the spiritual bap tism. After that, either thou, O bishop, or a presbyter that is under thee, shall in the solemn form name over them the Father, and Son, and Holy Spirit, and shall dip them in the water; and let a deacon receive the man, and a deaconess the woman, that so the conferring of this inviolable seal may take place with a becoming decency. And after that, let the bishop anoint those that are baptized with ointment" (*Constitutions of the Holy Apostles,* Book III, Section II, On Deacons and Deaconesses, the Rest of the Clergy, and on Baptism).

23. See the Nicene Creed.

24. "All Eastern Rite members should know and be convinced that they can and should always preserve their lawful liturgical rites and their established way of life, and that these should not be altered except by way of an appropriate and organic development. Easterners themselves should honor all these things with the greatest fidelity. Besides, they should acquire an ever greater knowledge and a more exact use of them. If they have improperly fallen away from them because of circumstances of times or personage, let them take pains to return to their ancestral ways" (*Orientalium Ecclesiarum* (Decree on the Catholic Churches of the Eastern Rite), §6).

25. Both priest and deacon recite the Prayer of Ephrem. Making a prostration, they begin in a low voice:

"Lord, Master of my life, grant that I may not be infected with the spirit of slothfulness and acquisitiveness, with the spirit of ambition and vain talking."

They rise, then make another prostration:

"Grant instead to me your servant the spirit of purity and humility, the spirit of patience and neighborly love."

They rise, then make a third prostration:

"O Lord and King, bestow upon me the grace of being aware of my sins and of not thinking evil of those of my brethren."

They rise, and continue aloud:

"For You are blessed for ever and ever."

All: "Amen."

And, making a reverence each time, the priest and deacon say:

"O God, be propitious to me a sinner and have mercy on me." (Twelve times)

And, making a final prostration, they repeat:

"Yes, O Lord and King, bestow upon me the grace of being aware of my sins and of not thinking evil of those of my brethren."

This prayer is taken from the Liturgy of the Presanctified Gifts found in *Byzantine Daily Worship* (Allendale, NJ: Alleluia Press), 1969.

26. "The Catholic Church holds in high esteem the institutions, liturgical rites, ecclesiastical traditions and the established standards of the Christian life of the Eastern Churches, for in them, distinguished as they are for their venerable antiquity, there remains conspicuous the tradition that has been handed down from the Apostles through the Fathers and that forms part of the divinely revealed and undivided heritage of the universal Church" (*Orientalium Ecclesiarum* (Decree on the Catholic Churches of the Eastern Rite), §1).

27. See *Ut Unam Sint,* ¶54.